Our Selves

BY THE SAME AUTHOR PUBLISHED BY PROTEA BOOK HOUSE:
Klip en klei
Die neukery met die appelboom
Pots and Poetry and other essays
Oor gode en afgode

Our Selves

Martin Versfeld

Protea Book House
Pretoria
2010

Our Selves – Martin Versfeld

First edition, first impression in 1979 by David Philip
Second edition, first impression in 2010 by Protea Book House

PO Box 35110, Menlo Park, 0102
1067 Burnett Street, Hatfield, Pretoria
8 Minni Street, Clydesdale, Pretoria
protea@intekom.co.za
www.proteaboekhuis.com

Editor: Iolandi Pool
Cover design: Hanli Deysel
Typography: 11.5 on 17 pt ZapfCalligr by Hanli Deysel
Printed and bound: Creda, Cape Town

© 2010 Ruth Versfeld
ISBN 978-1-86919-371-3

All rights reserved. No part of this book may be reproduced or transmitted in any form or by any electronic or mechanical means, including photocopying and recording, or by any other information storage or retrieval system, without written permission from the publisher.

Contents

Introduction:

GRASPING THE TRUTH FROM WHERE WE ARE

Ernst Wolff 7

1 OUR SELVES 43
2 THE EGO IN INDIAN THOUGHT 62
3 THE IMPORTANCE OF BEING HUMAN 74
4 THE DESIRABILITY OF DESIRE 92
5 THE YIN AND THE YANG IN CHRISTIAN CULTURE .. 110
6 IDEALISM AND MATERIALISM IN ETHICS 136
7 THE HUMAN VISION 161
8 ON JUSTICE AND HUMAN RIGHTS 173
9 REFLECTIONS ON EVOLUTIONARY KNOWLEDGE 190
10 ST THOMAS, NEWMAN
   AND THE EXISTENCE OF GOD 233

Bibliography 271

Grasping the truth from where we are

1. INTRODUCTION: FLUX, STABILITY AND WHERE WE ARE

Who we as humans are is arguably the most pervasive theme in the thought of Martin Versfeld. In the concluding remarks to his *An essay on the metaphysics of Descartes* (1940),* he deplores Descartes's egocentric self that is isolated from body, others and world; that is to say where any relation to them remains merely accidental to what the ego essentially is. Half a century later he chose the title *Sum* – I am – for a selection of his essays, which serves as "a sort of biography". Situating this thought between the rejection of Descartes and the adoption of Socrates and Thomas Aquinas, he favours the "consonance" of oneself with oneself, others and the environment.† Roughly in-between, his 1971 inaugural lecture at the University of Cape Town is devoted to the Socratic quest of "knowing thyself" and was chosen to open a book entitled *Persons*.‡ When the first page of *Our Selves* then opens with the So-

---

*　London: Methuen and Co., 1940, chapter XI, especially pp. 148–150. This book is the published version of Versfeld's doctoral thesis, completed in Glasgow in 1934, and represents his earliest independent work.

†　Cf. *Sum. Selected works. 'n Keur uit sy werke*. Cape Town: The Carrefour Press, p. 7.

‡　"The Socratic spirit", in *Persons*, Cape Town: Buren, 1971, pp. 1–15.

cratic call to know yourself, and frames this straightaway by a critique of Descartes's notion of the ego and approval of some detail on the thought of Augustine and Aquinas, one easily recognises the architect of this building by its façade, the design of which – as Versfeld explains – is an autobiographical act (OS 164).

Yet, such an architectural image may attribute more stability and structure to this collection of ten essays than it really has. By the time they were published together in 1979, some of them already had an eventful career behind them. "On justice and human rights" first appeared in 1960* and could therefore have been completed two decades before *Our Selves*. "The human vision" might be equally old.† Some essays tell a different story. "St Thomas, Newman and the existence of God" appeared in 1967,‡ and a version of it was later chosen to become a chapter in *A saraband of the sons of God*.§ But *A saraband of the sons of God* never saw the light of day. Two other essays from *Our Selves*, "Reflections on evolutionary knowledge"** and "On justice and human rights" were set to become two of the

---

*   Published in *Acta Juridica* 1, 1960.
†   The fact that a typed copy of this essay appears with other essays of the late 1950s (in the Versfeld collection in the University of Cape Town's archive, file 59) allows fixing its date of writing with some uncertainty in the same period.
‡   *New Scholasticism* 41, Winter 1967.
§   The selection of essays on authors such as Augustine, Rousseau, Kolbe, Chesterton, Aquinas and Newman was probably compiled around 1971 and can be found in the UCT archive, files 155, 156 & 157.
**   Published initially in the *International philosophical Quarterly*, vol. 5 of May 1965.

five chapters of Versfeld's *Towards an existential political philosophy*.* But *Towards an existential political philosophy* was never published either. Furthermore, whereas some of the separate chapters were, then, previously assigned to be read in association with chapters other than their neighbours in *Our Selves*, there is reason to believe that "The desirability of desire" was initially not planned to be included in *Our Selves* and three other essays were.† From this information it is manifest that *Our Selves* had been simmering for a long time before it was dished up in its current format and we can understand why Versfeld could later say that "For me, making soup is rather like writing; my mind is a rag-bag, bits occasionally cohering to form some sort of unity."‡ Ten essays, amended over two decades and flowing into an occasional coherence, would come closer to a description of this collection.

This detail on the boiling process from which *Our Selves* originated is not of marginal interest to understanding the book, in fact, it confronts us with its central concern. And if it is permissible to remind guests of the laurel leaves that

---

*   The complete typescript of this book is in the UCT archive, file 68. It seems most probable that it was compiled somewhere after 1966 and before 1972. The three other essays of this book would have been "Metaphysics in our time", "Augustine and the politics of time" and "Law and the idea of the contemporary" – they can be read in other publications.

†   This claim is made on the basis of the content of file 136 in the UCT archive: it contains a mix of manuscripts, typescripts and article print-offs for nine of the ten chapters of *Our Selves*, plus three other essays.

‡   *Food for thought. A philosopher's cookbook*, Cape Town: Carrefour Press, [1983]1991.

infuse a dish, but are removed before serving, I may cite from one of the discarded passages that was intended to give flavour to two of the essays of the current volume and claim that it significantly informs the thought of *Our Selves*:

> All things pass, as Theresa of Avila so often said, and though we reach out from the flux to grasp a stability which is the common aspiration of all men, yet the point from which we reach out is different for every man and for every generation, borne on as they are by the sweep of the creative process. We see the truth from where we are.*

According to this noteworthy clarification, the process by which this book of Versfeld was formed can be said to bear the traces (cf. OS 202f) of the flux of time – the time of the personal life of Martin to whom these texts refer retrospectively. Through the eventful formation of the book its author continually attempted to make sense of his own contingent situatedness and in this way persistently affirmed the soundness of aspiring to find "a stability". "A stability" is not the perspectiveless, one-size-fits-all truth, but a truth that belongs to someone, that in turn belongs to a social reality, and by extension, to a history and to a world and ultimately to a "creative process". Conversely, this is not an *à la carte* truth chosen at will either, but a

---

*   Cited from the second paragraph of the "Preamble" to *Towards an existential political philosophy* (UCT archive, file 68).

creative force in which one can participate – such is the stability that Versfeld will attempt to uphold and illuminate in dialogue with a series of authors, represented in this citation by St Theresa.

Since all of the themes of the book are in one way or another related to this basic orientation with respect to "where we are" it would be in order to say something more about it.

2. ANTHROPOLOGY AS FIRST PHILOSOPHY

Our Selves is a book of philosophy and it is therefore of no mean importance to notice what Versfeld girds himself for when he puts on the philosopher's mantle: "Philosophy ought to start with anthropology in the Continental use of the term. What comes first is not theory of knowledge, but the problem of the being of man", he writes in the opening sentence of "The importance of being human", and adds "We shall appreciate this better the more clearly we see how anthropomorphic all our knowledge is" (OS 74). If one counts well, it follows this remark that philosophy, even philosophical anthropology, comes always second at best: first is the problem of being human, then comes reflection on this problem. Subsequently one does best to start philosophy by thinking about the human being and not about epistemology, since one risks failing to see how the problem of being human shapes knowledge. Another way of putting it would be to say that all philosophical claims, in fact all truth claims, derive their nature, meaning and significance from their setting in human life. The same holds for whatever one can desire to do with truths: conducting politics, developing technologies, promoting culture, and even practising religion.

Hence the need for a book that contemplates ourselves as human beings. Now Versfeld chose for the title of his collection of essays to separate "our" and "selves". "Selves" is a noun, the plural of "self", which the reader will see can be used with a small or capital S, and the title qualifies "selves" by the possessive pronoun in the first person plural, "our". These snippets of linguistic elucidation suggest that there are more than one self for each human being, the association with which is to be understood as a kind of "possession" or "having" and that one does better to consider this having of selves as something that concerns *us*, and not only *me*. In this way the title leads to the central tenet of Versfeld's thought on the self: everybody has the choice between two divergent forms of existence, or to put it more bluntly: "we have two selves, and it is fatal to choose the wrong one".* When Versfeld roots philosophy in the problem of being human, he therefore derives the significance of all aspects of reality – be it political, technological, cultural or religious – from the decisive question concerning the quality of one's self and of the ways in which you have your self with others.

If the one option is for the I, self or ego and a life guided by grasping desire and *samsara*, the other option is for the

---

* Martin Versfeld, *Pots and Poetry and other essays*. Pretoria: Protea Boekhuis, [1985]2009, p. 70.

real self, the Self, the person that exercises generous desire and follows the Tao or finds union with God. The reader will not find it difficult to trace the detail of this distinction throughout the book. Yet, one should guard against seeing this as a simple split between a narrow and broad way. We should rather see two modifications of the same human existence, the difference being located in the variation of the attitude one adopts towards one's incarnation in a body, a society and an environment. A first approximation to these two attitudes is provided by the existential distinction between recognition and disregard for transitive *being*: I am my body, I don't merely inhabit it (OS 79ff), I am with others, they are not merely added to me (OS 146f), I am my world, it doesn't merely contain me (OS 180). And hence, any attitude towards human existence that disregards these aspects of one's existence by reducing the human being to either mind or body, and humanity to a collection of individuals or by alienating the world from the people, is calling for personal, sociopolitical and environmental pathologies associated with the distortion of the real self.

But one comes closer to Versfeld's sophisticated reinterpretation of incarnation in *Our Selves*, by recalling the possessive pronoun in the title: "our", which applies to both of our selves. As a matter of fact, Versfeld reveals that the transitive notion of being can itself be considered a form of having – having as something more primitive than legal ownership (OS 186); *having as attachment through desire or love*. Our desires constitute the very nature of our temporality that is lived as much bodily as mentally and therefore are the energy of the delight one can have in oneself (OS 49f, 53). Desires are "post-social" – we are directed at the world in a socially constituted manner – and the quality of our loves determines the quality of our relations to others (OS 51, 94). And if life is "an activity which makes things surrounding the living being relevant" (OS 175), it is because through loving and desiring we are incarnated in a sphere of relevance; one possesses one's self by possessing the world (OS 178). Having, as the nature of one's loving or desiring, is what makes a self, whether it is more the real and decisive Self or the superficial and pathological mutation of it. Consequently, sinking into, or hardening into the grasping ego is then at the root of the sociopolitical misery presented throughout the book.

Despite this schematisation of two attitudes towards one's existence which is needed for the diagnostic criticism of the ego, nothing is further from Versfeld's intention than a course moralism based on a denial of the difficult link between the two selves. Finding the true and decisive Self cannot mean to bring an end to the ego, since the very attempt to escape from the small self is itself an act of perseverance in the small self or the desperate effort to escape the grasping ego and the deformed world that its action creates, is still a grasping of the ego.* If, accord-

---

* Or again "[d]oging out of *samsara* is a *samsaric* dodge", Martin Versfeld, *St. Augustine's Confessions and City of God*. Cape Town: Carrefour, 1990, p. 10.

ing to Buddhism: "Nirvana is *not* total extinction but the extinction of the grasping ego" (OS 57), Versfeld still affirms the Buddhists saying: "let your *samsara* be your *nirvana*" (OS 106). Or to translate the same principle into more Augustinian parlance: "at the heart of every desire, no matter how sinful, there is a seed of the divine radiance which can be set free" (OS 101) and hence therapy consists, not of uprooting, but elevating warped desires (OS 104). That is why Versfeld could claim that the essence of the most severe religious practice, ascesis, "is not struggling or straining but relaxing into what we are" (OS 71).*

This is an important point, especially when bearing in mind those people for whom this talk of finding a true self might sound too much like torturous abnegation or misty esoterica. Seeking the true self is not levitating above the common reality of daily life, but the submerging into the reality of that life itself: even in things as plain as washing dishes (OS 50).† One could simply say that the true self is "our concrete individual being historically situated in the world" (OS 249). This particular situatedness is exactly the

---

* This is the locus in *Our Selves* in which to look for an elucidation of the idea that "the secular is the miraculous", what I have called elsewhere the analogical difference or the analogical spark (see the discussion in § 6.3 of my introduction to the second edition of Versfeld's *Oor gode en afgode*. Pretoria: Protea Boekhuis, [1948]2010). For examples of this philosophical fingerprint of Versfeld in *Our Selves*, see OS 50, 60, 69f, 103, 106, 132.

† See also *St. Augustine's Confessions and City of God*. op. cit. p. 10: "Spirituality is not found by withdrawal from the world but by the indrawal of the world."

fact that has to be assumed in order to think (OS 249) or as Versfeld elaborates: "We must, then, accept ourselves as we are, limited and embodied, and really connected with other beings including sensible beings. We seek to make sense of what we so accept not for the sake of any arbitrary assumption to be proved but simply in order to be able to accept ourselves as we are." (OS 259). This is the "where we are" from which we see the truth (as in the citation discussed at the end of §1), but since it is the never completely recoverable source of relevance of thought, it will forever remain a mystery (OS 157). Hence, Versfeld's assertion concerning philosophy in his inaugural lecture: "I must confess at once that I do not know what philosophy is. This sometimes embarrasses me before the innocence of students, but not before those who have come to realise that the things by which we live are the things about which we know least. We do not know what life is, or what knowing is, or what truth and goodness are. Or if we do know we can't say it [...]."* Anthropology as first philosophy is philosophy that thrives from *that by which we live*; from the abyssal and unknown depths of our existence (OS 128).

3. TRADITIONS AND CULTURAL CRITICISM

One has to recognise that this decentring or unsettling of philosophical reflection by the singular human life calls for an appropriate relation to the (often one-sided) his-

---

* Martin Versfeld, *Persons*. Cape Town: Buren, 1971, p. 1.

tory of thought by which any contemporary philosopher has been schooled to think. This is the reason for the surprising intertwinement of traditions of thought from which Versfeld draws in *Our Selves*: first the Greeks (especially Plato, e.g. OS 46, 51f, 99f, 188f), then Biblical theology (e.g. OS 111ff) and its medieval reception (which is already a combination of the former two), especially that of Augustine and Aquinas (see for instance Augustine's theory of desires, OS 94ff, and Aquinas's of knowledge, OS 212ff). But *Our Selves* opens with a burst of Oriental wisdom – especially Buddhism (most of the first two chapters of OS), but also Taoism (OS 54, 87, 93, 133f) and a bit of Hinduism (e.g. OS 45, 62, 64ff) and Jewish mysticism (e.g. OS 93f, 103f, 109).* Lastly, there is a very distinct line of existentialism and/or phenomenology, which is quite surprising if one considers Versfeld's general critique of modern philosophy.† All of these strands are woven together

---

*   Placing Jewish mysticism in the same basket as the variety of expressions of Eastern wisdom is somewhat artificial. However, Versfeld had the impression, at least from the mid-1970s that he witnessed a boom in Western interest for Oriental thought and later clearly associated Jewish mysticism with it. In fact, we are thinking primarily of Baal Shem Tov, often in Buber's rendering of his life. See especially "A Western sunrise" in *Pots and Poetry*. op. cit. pp. 54–61.

†   Readers of Versfeld's *The mirror of the philosophers* (London/New York: Sheed & Ward, 1960) will remember that he explained that his friend Johan Degenaar compelled him to rethink his formulation of an up to then primarily Neo-Thomistic and Neo-Augustinian philosophy (p. 43). Whereas this acknowledgment leads to a discussion on Kierkegaard, and Versfeld retains a certain distance with respect to phenomenological interpretations of Christianity, it is probably to this book that his appreciation for the phenomenological tradition should be traced.

in an intricate dialogue where Versfeld does his best to respect the differences even while driving at his most central idea: from all of them we can learn concerning the perennial philosophy (OS 160, 173), from all of them there is substantial instruction to be drawn from which one could say that it fulfils the function of philosophy "not to discover new truths but to explicitate the truth which is given with us in our own existence." (OS 260).

If there is a need for this development in philosophy, it is because of the particular situation in which Western modernity has brought itself and large parts of the world in its wake. This calamity – which is nothing but the negative diagnosis persistent in all of Versfeld's work* and the background against which his preoccupation for what we are is to be understood – is the nominalist revolution and the decay of the medieval unity.

One can read the features of this process of decay at different places throughout *Our Selves* (see in particular OS 118ff). The tendency to separate body and mind is accompanied by overconfidence in the capacity to see what is going on in the mind, as well as the fragmentation of human reason and the unrealistic emphasis on certain aspects of this reason (OS 119). The separation of mind and body is replicated on a larger scale in the tendency to exaggeratedly separate society and nature (OS 118). With this is linked the excessive development of the masculine urge to dominate, enforced by science and technology (OS 121f)

---

*   As already in *Oor gode en afgode. op. cit.*, p. 40.

and the reduction of natural and human processes to mechanics (OS 126f). This development, supported by advertisement, fuels consumption (both of which result in the widespread distortion of desires) and therefore stands in the service of capitalism (OS 119). The latter requires asceticism in service of this process and concomitant individualism, which in turn facilitates the exploitation of nature and other human beings and the reduction of value to monetary value.

I leave the reader to discover how Versfeld develops the connection between these phenomena – and to decide to what degree they could be said to be harmful developments with respect to the European medieval condition of life.

What has to be noted is that all of these phenomena are presented as sociopolitical symptoms of disregard for the perennial philosophy, but more profoundly, of the illness of the grasping ego gone rampant. These symptoms of the decay brought about by modernity can equally be traced in the work of such modern philosophers as Descartes, Bacon, Machiavelli, Rousseau, Hobbes, Hume, Kant, Hegel and Marx – and they form a tradition of thought from which Versfeld wishes to save the contemporary world.

If there is in *Our Selves* a complex dispute between proponents of Greek, Christian and Oriental thought on the one hand and the modern philosophers on the other, it is not as a childish fight of schools but for the sake of the health of society.

This point may be overlooked, since so much in the book is developed around the question of the two selves. But careful examination will reveal that the human being in its society with others and with the environment is equally at stake in *Our Selves*. Not only does the violence of modern sociopolitical life form the diagnosis to which Versfeld responds, but as he learned from Augustine, ethics and politics should be seen to have immediate mutual implications (OS 96), which could be traced in our reflection on desire and on justice (OS 96, 173).* The reason for the indissociable link between ethics and politics is the sociopolitical constitution of the world (OS 201). Moreover, the wellbeing of the body politic, a just social fibre, is created by the collective effect of healthy personal relations (OS 183).

4. USING A THORN TO TAKE OUT A THORN, AND THROWING BOTH AWAY

In accordance with his view that philosophy is not intent on discovering new truths, but on the explicitation of what is given (as explained above), one doesn't find the author of *Our Selves* working on the construction of a novel philo-

---

* Writing his review (in *African Book Publishing Record* VI, 3/4, probably 1979) of *Our Selves* from South Carolina, Daniel Sabia seemed to miss the significance of this point. Although the reviewer understands the enrootedness of all the concerns of Versfeld's book in human existence, he fails to see that the entire ethics of the self developed in these essays is a politics of the self as access to the society and world in which the self is to live.

sophical system. He attempts much rather to call us back to something from which we cannot escape and of which he is not the author. The value of his writing is situated in translating the perennial philosophy for a specific context, according to the needs of this context. Hence the independence of Versfeld's thought consists precisely in writing from where he is.

Two salient features of his manner of working follow on from this orientation and situation of his work – let's call them reduction and detachment.

4.1 REDUCTION – USING A SECOND THORN

There can be no doubt about the central importance of religious thought – in particular the Catholic thought of God – in the entirety of Versfeld's works. And yet, it is not so simple to say flatly that his philosophy is Christian. Versfeld is quite clear on this in an earlier draft for the first paragraph of "The yin and the yang in Christian culture" (OS chapter 5): "Being known to be officially a Catholic in the regions where I live, I am sometimes asked: you're a Catholic, aren't you? I can never reply without a considerable degree of hesitation. I have pondered over this hesitation. I have come to the conclusion that this pondering has sufficient significance to be made public. § This isn't quite as personal as it sounds. We are all under the influence of the Christian ethic and spirituality. We inevitably go on being Christian as Chinese go on being Confucian, no matter what sea-changes have occurred. The Marxist, for instance, continues to be dynamised, of historical necessity, by much of what he explicitly rejects. You can take stock of where you are, but you cannot step out of it."* In other words, for Versfeld, thought about being a Christian, and his own in particular, has to acknowledge the general cultural shaping it has undergone by a certain Christian heritage, but has to do so in two divergent ways: one that recognises the failures, weaknesses and violence of this tradition, the other that explores the true core of assumed Christianity. We find a number of forms of existence of Christianity that are rejected by Versfeld and the reader can learn much of the author's cultural criticism from this: fundamentalist and moralist Protestantism (OS 120), the body-despising, institution-rejecting and business-minded Puritan individualism (OS 89f, 123), some of the "superficial fools who write books on apologetics" (OS 248), of course Cartesianism, where God comes only to a solitary, ahistorical, disincarnate and world-doubting mind (OS 249, 258) and the political compromise and moral policing of some popes and the curia (OS 113, 116).

But just as it is, therefore, not that simple to say that Versfeld is a proponent of Christianity, so it is, in his mind, not evident to deny a certain Christianity that energises his non-Christian contemporaries. What Versfeld intends to do is to find what is precious in both confessing and cultural Christianity. However, this statement should be

---

* In UCT archive, file 135. Although these two paragraphs are crossed out, I consider them to state in a more personal and specific manner, what is written in more general terms in the final version of the text, and partially overlaps with it (OS 52).

qualified, since for Versfeld it is not a matter of Christianity as opposed to other religions (as can be seen in particular in Chapters 1 & 2), nor of faith in opposition to reason (see in particular Chapters 8 & 9). In fact, the other religions and the use of reason are vital for calling us back to that something from which his thought draws, "that by which we live" (or ought to), that which the perennial philosophy attempts to explicitate truthfully.

The different traditions of religion and thought from which Versfeld borrows in *Our Selves* all serve to lead us back to this mysterious and elusive core. It is not to introduce a new and truer thought or religions that Versfeld engages with Buddhism or Taoism, but "for many of us at any rate, it would be wiser if these Eastern ideas served to remind us of things that have been forgotten or have gone stale in our own tradition, and brought new life to them" (OS 132) – this "own tradition" being our Christian past of which we cannot rid ourselves (OS 110, 132, 255f). Buddhism puts the taste back into Christianity. But the service can be rendered in the opposite direction too: "Those who think that Buddhism contains the answer to all their problems, fail to see the strength of their own tradition. While Buddhist pundits were hairsplitting grasping desire into many dozens of variety, Western thinkers were analysing the political consequences of grasping desire. The foremost was St Augustine…" (OS 96) – and apart from the instruction on the political implications of desire that Augustine can give his Buddhist colleagues, he shows his strength by calling to our minds the fact that distorted desires do not point the way to eliminating desire, but to the need for elevating them (OS 104). For Versfeld, instead of this debate leading eventually to the elimination of one of the parties, the reconstructed discussion serves rather to enhance the searching effort: since "Every man is naturally in the truth – a Zenist would say that he is a Buddha; a Christian that he is in the image of God" (OS 156), the mutual contradictions remind us of the provisional character of both and should encourage continual discussion by which we are led back to this non-propositional truth in which we live.*

Let it immediately be added that philosophy has its voice to add to this chorus. Having transcended the strictures of the materialism-idealism debate, contemporary philosophy finds the unity between humans and their world, and as a result can help us to better understand Oriental thought (OS 160). Particularly remarkable is the role attributed to philosophy with regard to Aquinas: his proofs of the existence of God "must be given an existential interpretation" (OS 251) and from the context one

---

*   The complex interplay between traditions should guard the reader against biased presentations, such as reducing Versfeld to his appropriation of Oriental thought – as was done by the anonymous reviewer of *Our Selves* in "Mirror of enlightenment", *The Cape Times*, 12 May 1979. In his review of *Our Selves*, Hennie Rossouw is more precise by saying that Versfeld doesn't plead for a "spiritual emigration" out of the Western tradition and rather seeks to affirm one's embeddedness in that heritage by means of Oriental wisdom (see "Versfeld – filosoof met eie boodskap" in *Die Burger*, 12 July 1979). But this holds, of course, only for those standing in the Western tradition.

should understand this as an existential, phenomenological interpretation. The fact that Versfeld undertakes this existentialisation of Aquinas by means of the Catholic philosophy of John Henry Newman, is of secondary importance.

The spirit of this confrontation of different traditions seems to me perfectly captured in the phrase: "to go back to the perennial philosophy", in which the latter is immediately defined in terms of the meaningful relatedness of people to a world (OS 160), i.e. as itself leading one back to what precedes philosophy. Versfeld's way of going about consists of leading his reader and his dialogical partners back from each of these spectator views (and especially the modernist absolutisation of spectator views) to the view or rather the fact of being a participator in a world, in other words to our true selves.* It is only from participation in existence that one can find one's own humanity and world *meaningful* (OS 264). By contrast, philosophy that starts from doubt withdraws the thinker from the personal, social and natural world that makes that thinker into a person (OS 180); by recognising the practical situatedness and the meaningfulness of one's situation one

---

*   I have underscored the position of a certain influence of phenomenology on Versfeld, not only because the notion of leading back (reduction as *re-ducere*) is a central notion operating in phenomenology, but also because reduction is charged with coping with the relation between the self as spectator and the self as participator. See Rudolf Bernet in "La réduction phénoménologique et la double vie du sujet" in: *La vie du sujet. Recherches sur l'interprétation de Husserl dans la phénoménologie*. Paris: PUF, 1994, pp. 5–36.

can think about things that matter. Hence the superiority of Aquinas over Descartes (OS 249), or Newman over Russel (OS 254). Hence also the importance of Aquinas's assertion that the human being has intellect and hands (OS 184, 187, 220, 251). It seems to me that the combination of intellect and hands amounts for Versfeld to practical reason or prudence (OS 182, 264) – i.e. reason as physically, historically, socially and environmentally situated and which seems to be the root of anything that could be called rational or reasonable for Versfeld.* Hence the importance of the life that supports an argument – who one is, or rather, what kind of life one has, matters at least as much as what one's opinion is. In fact, philosophy is for Versfeld first of all a way of life, as has been affirmed with force by Pierre Hadot, and one could rightfully claim that the message of *Our Selves* is the call for the art of coming home.†

But by working towards the confluence of these traditions and carefully choosing which aspects to highlight and which parts to make echo with others, has Versfeld not in fact created his own theory of human existence and

---

* While avoiding for current purposes extensive comparisons between Versfeld and other philosophers, one can hardly omit noting the striking similarity between the centrality of a metaphysics in which all categories of being are reduced from a phenomenological reinterpretation of Aristotle's notion of *phronesis* (prudence) as in Heidegger and Versfeld's existentialisation of Aquinas with the help of Newman in order to place the practical reason as the source of all intelligence.

† As Hennie Rossouw pointed out in his discussion of *Our Selves* in "Die kuns van die lewe is om tuis te kom. Gedagtes oor die filosofie van Martin Versfeld" *Tydskrif vir Geesteswetenskappe*, 1996, 36/1, pp. 11–20, here pp.18–19.

made it the universal code of entry into meaningful human existence?

4.2 DETACHMENT – THROWING BOTH THORNS AWAY

Versfeld answers the objection above very explicitly: "It may, of course, be retorted that in this chapter I have been theorising myself, and simply putting up an alternative construction. I could reply in the words of a Buddhist that Buddhism was using a thorn to take out a thorn, after which one throws both away. […] [W]hat I have tried to do is to point to a moral fact rather than explain it. It remains a mystery to me. If I have called your attention to yourselves you can forget about me." (OS 157). If the sociopolitical evils of the modern world and the philosophical expressions that supported it implicitly or not, represent the first thorn, then all of the traditions which Versfeld deploys, and certainly his own work, represent a second thorn, that is destined to be discarded with the first one... but not without having used it first. And not without the conviction (or the assumption, OS 248) that by doing so, something of decisive importance is laid bare. But have we not seen from the beginning that this something decisive, this mystery, is "our concrete individual being historically situated in the world" (OS 249)? Has this concrete existence not been expounded as the most primitive form of having? Why then speak of detachment and not rather of attachment?

To be true, these questions lead us to the apparent paradox that "the only attachment is detachment" (OS 104).

By being "intellect and hands", human beings penetrate into their surrounding environment and establish ties of relevance with that which they are not (OS 176) and it is exactly by appropriating a world in this manner that one becomes a person (OS 180). Accordingly, attachment is epistemologically and practically given (OS 105, 185). This seems to me to be ultimately the significance of Versfeld's ceaseless insistence that the basis of acting in the world is the fact that the world is already in us (e.g. OS 79, 85, 137, 146, 177, 211). One could reformulate: that an environment has meaning to someone, is what makes it possible to act. Therefore, the speaking about detachment is a "spiritual counsel" (OS 105) not to become so obsessed by the people and things with whom we interact that we lose sight of the ways in which we are meaningfully woven into our environment of people, things and nature. Detachment, therefore, doesn't serve to withdraw from the world or to dissolve into a bland state of apathy, but rather to reassume the meaning that constitutes us as persons by "relaxing into what we are" (OS 71). It is a major persuasion of *Our Selves*, and probably of all of Versfeld's work, that what we are, is given to us, proceeds from divine generosity and comes to us as the procession of the creatures created by God (OS 105f, 108, 185). If detachment is relaxing into the flow of time initiated by this creative process, then finding the true self means acting "directly out of what we are" (OS 154). That is why "the saint's detachment is really a higher form of attachment" (OS 105) and therefore ethics has everything to do with creativity and not that much with rules, in Versfeld's mind. In other words, moral judgment is for him less the application of principles or ideals and much rather a matter of spontaneity – and on this Christian, Oriental and contemporary existentialist thinkers would concur (OS 154f). One could say that the ethics of detachment is an ethics of love, since "love is creatively spontaneous".*

But I have announced the theme of detachment by saying that it forms part of Versfeld's way of working. By describing what detachment entails for one's life, I have not lost my thread, but prepared the context from which detachment as a manner of philosophising draws its meaning. We can observe in a number of ways how Versfeld attempts to detach himself from his very writing even when writing. The interference of different traditions of thought could be considered the first of these: it might be that elements from them are woven together in a supportive manner to form the "second thorn", but this can be done only at the expense of whatever claim to exclusivity any of them might have. The value of Versfeld's trade is submitted to a similar relativisation: detached dishwashing is in final consideration more valuable than expressing one's ego by writing a tome of philosophy. This means that philosophy is reduced to recalling or pointing to truth, instead of containing it – "If I have called your attention to yourselves you can forget about me." (OS 157). Humility, which is the basis of the cardinal virtues, is therefore certainly more

---

*   *Food for thought.* op. cit. p. 92.

than the style of presentation of one's writing or action – it is the act of detachment by which one affirms that one belongs to a world that is given, not self-made (OS 178ff).

Versfeld seems to drive the detachment of his philosophising to a climax in the last chapter of *Our Selves*, when he digresses on the nature of philosophy (OS 260f). The pretence of philosophy to discover new truths is discarded and the claim of a certain philosophical tendency to master its own hold on reason by methodological doubt is pushed aside in favour of drawing from naivety. In this sense philosophy thrives on a sort of stupidity (OS 55). Furthermore, instead of serious work or even serious creation, the first virtue of the metaphysician is now said to be play, understood as "conflict creatively controlled by a containing order" (OS 260). One can hardly miss how far Versfeld is on the road of detachment, when he – who insisted that philosophy starts with anthropology and adamantly affirmed the anthropomorphic nature of our knowledge – asserts that the human being is not only insignificant (OS 77f) and unknowable, but funny and elevates humour to the heart of philosophical seriousness. Kierkegaard is singled out as a thinker who "had the humorous sense of incongruity and the comic necessary for a metaphysician." (OS 261).

Readers of Versfeld's work of the 1980s might interpret his exquisite sense of humour as the licence of a retired professor who is fed-up with the discipline of academic writing. Perhaps this is not devoid of truth. But it would at least be equally plausible to see this turn of style as progress in his detachment. "Detaching yourself from things is a good old advice", the Catholic philosopher writes in an essay on "Mucking out" and continues: "If you chuck the Bible into the wastepaper basket, it proves perhaps that you have learned its most intimate lesson."*

5. QUESTIONING FROM WHERE WE ARE

If Versfeld confronts us with ourselves and the world in which we live, he can do so only by confronting us with himself. In this introduction I have attempted to show how he does this by highlighting a number of the most striking themes that run through this selection of essays and by interpreting their interconnection. A proper evaluation of the book can be undertaken only by considering it in all its complex and intricate detail – a pleasure to which I hasten to invite the reader. Thus, in conclusion, I shall merely suggest a number of questions – ensuing from the previous discussion – that might enhance the reader's attention when reading the book and contemplating its content.

Decisive for any reception of Versfeld's thought is the extent to which one considers his diagnosis of modernity convincing. The decay of the medieval unity, started by the nominalist revolution and developed fully in modernity, tends to be represented as grid for reading contemporary sociopolitical evils, as the historical manifestation

---

* See "Opruim" in *Die neukery met die appelboom en ander essays*. Pretoria: Protea Boekhuis, [1985]2009, p 30.

of the political implications of an Augustinian diagnosis of distorted desires. Versfeld surely suffers no shortage of examples to make the case for an ailing Western world, and when he goes so far as to consider Hitler to be "an inevitable phenomenon of a utilitarian rationalising society and a product of the Enlightenment" (OS 128), one has to acknowledge that he is in good company (think especially of the Critical Theorists of the Frankfurt School). Yet, one could wonder if more recognition and a snugger place in his philosophy of history are not due to other fruits of modernity. I think not only of the virtues of existentialist phenomenology (since he sings its praises in *Our Selves*), but more importantly the humanist cultural politics of the Enlightenment which (apart from whatever valid criticism one might want to formulate against it) should at least be credited for creating the intellectual climate and institutional support in which translations of and commentaries on the Upanishads, Lao-Tzu and Chuang-Tzu and the Buddhist masters (on which Versfeld's thought flourishes) could be made and is, additionally, responsible for creating the means by which to edit and distribute these and other texts, without which Versfeld's work would simply be impossible.

Conspicuous in Versfeld's encompassing outline of modern decay is the absence of the profusion of the arts. Surely one can trace very modernist characteristics in the different forms of artistic invention of this period, but I find it difficult to see the music of Bach, for instance, as a symptom of decay of anything. Or should one rather understand Versfeld to maintain that some modern sociopolitical tendencies are harmful and either motivated or testified to by modern philosophers, but that other typical modern phenomena are either good or at least harmless? But if this is the case, one will have to embark on a very tough search in Versfeld's text for the sources of this non-medieval (and non-Buddhist, non-Taoist, etc.) sources of wellbeing in modernity itself. Furthermore, if the decay of the medieval unity explains Hobbes and Descartes, what explains Kierkegaard and Nietzsche?* Or is it implied that modern culture is to be understood to carry some good despite itself, analogously to the deformed desires of which Versfeld says that they should not be uprooted but elevated, since they contain some good (OS 101, 104)?

Contrasting a philosophy that starts in doubt with one that seeks to excavate and explicitate meaning is not unacceptable (think for example of Versfeld's contemporary, Paul Ricoeur, who drew a similar distinction between interpretation as an exercise of suspicion and interpretation as recollection of meaning). But would one not risk succumbing to plain naivety if one were to practise a philosophy of the explicitation of meaning without confronting

---

* I have shown elsewhere that in Versfeld's very first development of his criticism of modernity, Nietzsche is exempt of criticism and rather co-opted as a diagnostic partner (see my introduction to *Oor gode en afgode*. op. cit. p. 22). This is repeated with only a slight deviation in *Our Selves*. Kierkegaard is subject to a harder reading, but Versfeld elevates him in *Our Selves* at least to the position of quite a good modernist philosopher.

the pre-formed meaning steadily to different varieties of doubt or suspicion? Now, since one can certainly not attribute such a basic naivety to Versfeld, is one then to conclude that the kind of suspicion generally required by our times, can be delivered with the help not of Marx, Freud, Nietzsche and company, but with other means such as an elaboration on Augustine's philosophy of desire? (That such a cultural criticism with alternative means is realisable, is amply illustrated in Versfeld's feminist critique of modern Christian culture in Chapter 5.) But still, the latter does seem to have left the tissue of meaning weaved by the real self's being in the world in a state of uncompromised innocence. There is for instance, according to Versfeld "often more wisdom in our bodies formed by the eternal Tao than in our minds" (OS 134). In other words, for Versfeld the true self is not a predator, it is truly innocent, and yet, at the same time, the true self is also the singular, historically formed and situated self. Subsequently, this line of interrogation ultimately leads to the heart of the thesis of *Our Selves*, since the reader will have to decide with what justice Versfeld can suppose that the true self to which Versfeld attempts to lead his readers (and himself) back and which is characterised by the exercise of balanced desires, is the same as the particular historically situated being of every individual. One could also ask if it is not imaginable that the ego could sometimes act as the first defence against the mysterious forces at work in the inscrutable depths in which the singular, historical self is constituted.

The answer to these questions will decisively influence one's idea of the desirability and success of Versfeld's project.

These reflections on modernity inevitably direct one to ponder the notion of the world in which we live, or as Versfeld would say, the place where we are. Now, I understood well that he has insisted that this world is not the sum of things around us, neither merely the sum of mental pictures that we have of it, but the incarnate living in a sphere of relevance. Yet this notion of the world cannot be thought without consideration for the things that happen to surround a specific person. Therefore, whereas one might easily go along with Versfeld's criticism of contemporary capitalism and consumerist society, it is less obvious to see where his philosophy of the true self would lead those people whose daily life is shaped by the way in which they are inescapably embedded in this historical context.

This matter becomes painful when one ponders on what it could mean to find your true self by relaxing into what you are, for people living under conditions of social injustice, where what one is, is constituted by structural injustice. It might be a drawback of all his recuperation of classical and medieval authors, that none of them wrote from or for the life in the big modern city and hence their wisdom – how rich in instruction it might be – doesn't occupy itself with the intricacies of having to live in such an environment. Consequently, the teaching of the true self can remain intact and the complicated question regarding practically living in the modern world is hidden under the carpet of a cultural criticism of modern society. Or should the reader rather accept that the nature of advice for true living is such that it cannot prescribe, and that *Our Selves* is an invocation to an ethic of prudence and spontaneity for which every agent has to take individual responsibility?

But the question concerning "where we are" also has an intellectual side: if one concedes to Versfeld's claim (as regards to medieval Christianity) that one cannot tear yourself from the spiritual tradition in which you are historically rooted – should it then not be admitted that three or four centuries of modern history suffice to form a tradition of its own, one from which it might be equally injurious to tear yourself? And if one lives in plural traditions, would it not be necessary to reflect on the relative importance, significance, desirability and influence of these respective traditions? One would also have to contemplate, when reading *Our Selves*, what the position is of traditions that are not named here. Are they omitted simply because Versfeld didn't have time to work on all of them, or is it that they make no significant contribution in calling us to who we are? Something should at least be made explicit about this – a demand that has over the last three decades of South African history only gained in importance. And then one could also ask questions about the traditions that Versfeld draws on with as much enthusiasm as creativity. One case in point: I certainly don't deny a philosopher's right to select from other thinkers what to take over and what not, but if one considers the kind of repeated criticism to which a political thinker like Hobbes is exposed, one cannot but be astounded that Versfeld, for whom the very political import of his philosophy of our two selves is structured by an Augustinian continuity between ethics and politics (OS 96), never even mentions that the latter's justification of violent opposition against the Donatists constitutes "the key witness for the theological justification for forcible conversions, the Inquisition and the holy war, against deviants of all kinds".* The reader will have to decide if the criticism of unevenhandedness against Versfeld's use of historical sources is valid and, if so, what the significance thereof is for his central arguments.

A last set of interesting questions with which to explore *Our Selves* concerns exactly the relation between ethics and politics. I simply accept Versfeld's insistence on the role that interpersonal relations play in weaving a social and even political fabric. However, it is something quite different to infer that the "great injustices are the cumulative expression of the injustices done in particular personal relationships" (OS 183). I cite this statement since it says a lot about a tendency in *Our Selves* to reduce political action to ethical action. The consequence of doing this is that a very heavy load of decision making, also with the sight on political justice, is placed on the individual (cf.

---

* See Hans Küng's discussion of this in his chapter on Augustine in *Great Christian thinkers*, London: SCM Press, 1994; citation p. 82.

OS 181ff). This fits awkwardly with his insistence on the primordial sociality of people. But then, it cannot be denied that this shift gives vigour to individual responsibility in the suppressive context of Apartheid South Africa, which could perhaps be said to have necessitated a shift in the balance from political to ethical initiative. One will have to decide to what extent his ethicopolitical convictions in *Our Selves* took shape in response to the particular historical circumstances and whether they could be considered appropriate for this situation and for ours. Furthermore, even when considering the importance of individual responsibility, one has to contemplate if the desiring ego wouldn't under certain circumstances fare at least equally well in obstructing injustice as a mindset of detachment.

If these questions succeed in plunging the reader in the lively flow of reflection of which *Our Selves* is a mid-way account, they have served their purpose. A mid-way account is indeed what this book is – not only because, as has been indicated in the introduction, this selection of essays document something of the life and evolution of their author, but also because the book represents an episode of the continual effort of the author to elevate from his own grasping ego to his true self. Pointing out the developing tensions and unsettled issues in the book doesn't amount to rejecting it, rather, by entering into vigorous contemplation with these essays, the reader will be questioned, and challenged, by the development of a singular human being in his efforts to find his real self, to find *nirvana* in his particular *samsara*. Besides, the reader that looks to philosophy for a soup that has no strange aftertaste, will die of hunger.

ERNST WOLFF
UNIVERSITY OF PRETORIA
SEPTEMBER 2010

'Every man has forgotten who he is. One may understand the cosmos, but never the ego; the self is more distant than any star. Thou shalt love the Lord thy God; but thou shalt never know thyself. We are all under the same mental calamity; we have all forgotten our names. We have all forgotten what we really are. All that we call common sense and rationality and practicality and positivism only means that for certain dead levels of our life we forget that we have forgotten. All that we call spirit and art and ecstasy only means that for one awful instant we remember that we forget.' – *G.K. Chesterton*

'The law for the development of the self with respect to knowledge, in so far as it is true that the self becomes the self, is this, that the increasing degree of knowledge corresponds with the degree of self-knowledge, that the more the self knows, the more it knows itself. If this does not occur, then the more knowledge increases, the more it becomes a kind of inhuman knowing, for the production of which man's self is squandered.' – *S. Kierkegaard*

'Behold thyself by inward optics, and the crystalline of thy soul.' – *Sir Thomas Browne*

'We carry with us the wonders which we seek without us; there is all Africa and her prodigies within us.' – *Sir Thomas Browne*

'I can't explain *myself*, I'm afraid, Sir, said Alice, because I'm not myself, you see.' – *Lewis Carroll*

1 : Our Selves

The experience of philosophy, of practical life, and of history leads to an ever-growing conviction that at the root of the human condition lies the health and sickness of the self. Socrates said, "Know yourself," and St Augustine counsels self-knowledge as a duty owed to God. To arrive at this knowledge or its object remains very difficult. I remember a student who barged into my room one day, saying, "Sir, I want to know myself!" I wish I could remember how I dealt with the situation. Again, a girl stopped me in the corridor, saying, "Sir, how does one know philosophy?" And to this I replied that one couldn't, but that one could keep on trying. At present, many young people are trying to lead an authentic existence. To such a one I said, "Stop bothering; it is drinking this cup of tea." These problems are all ego-problems, questions raised by the rational ego, and concerning the rational ego.

Descartes maintained that one could have a clear and distinct idea of the self, which for him is the mind, an unfortunate position which has declined with the ebbing away of rationalism. St Thomas Aquinas, on the other hand, maintained that things were intrinsically intelligible in proportion to their place in the scale of being. Since God was very Being, God was the most intelligible of all that is. But the only intelligence equal to the being of God is his own intelligence. God escapes our intelligences just because he is extremely intelligible, and the greatest knowledge we can have of him is to know that we do not know him.

Human beings are embodied beings who know things by the hands and the senses. Hence men think most accurately about bodies. Physics is a great science because it is so well proportioned to the mind of man. But the self of man himself partly escapes his own intelligence. He is in himself more intelligible than bodies, but relatively to our knowing, less so. To know oneself one must give ignorance its place. There must always be some nescience in self-knowledge, just as there must be entire nescience in our knowledge of God. Even material things are dark to us, hidden from us, as St Augustine said. We do not have an angel's-eye or God's-eye view of them.

The self is *nobis occultissimum*, very much hidden, to use the words which St Augustine uses even about bodily things. Still, you can know more about the cortex than the cortex can know about you. The possession of self-consciousness is both a blessing and a curse. For one thing, it makes us know that we shall die, a knowledge which shadows all that we do, colours our sense of time, and poisons ageing for many people. We have to learn that our age today is the right age for us to be.

Self-knowledge is not the kind of knowledge which we have of this chair or this pen. It does not require that kind of subject-object relationship. However far we push that approach we shall remain ignorant of ourselves. We cannot abolish egoism by clear and distinct ideas. The self-enclosure of "I think" is the source of our misery.

Seeing this, some thinkers have interpreted the Biblical account of the Fall as the arrival of man at ego-consciousness, when he first finds arrival at the sense of individual existence fearful. Oriental thought arrived at this point very long ago. Thus we find in the *Brihadaranyaka Upanishad* (1.4.1–3) the following passage:

> Looking around he saw nothing else but himself. He first said 'I am' ... He was afraid ... Verily he had no delight, and henceforth the man who is so alone has no delight. He desired a second. In size he was as large as a man and a woman in close embrace. He split himself in two, and from hence man and wife came to be. Hence a human being is like a half-fragment.

This is a passage which inevitably reminds us of the speech of Aristophanes in the *Symposium* (which you should see, for it is too long to quote, and too amusing to contract).

Self-conscious man is fragmented man. When he became as God, knowing, he became divided from himself, from his God and from his garden. There was a barrier of fig leaves between him and his wife. Right and wrong began to plague him. The knowledge by which he knew himself was not the Logos, but the origin of a separateness which gave rise to a morality with which he built up the world as *maya*. It is not only selfishness which must be overcome, but ego-consciousness. We are committed to a desire and pursuit of the whole, in which we seek to recapture our original integrity, which is not to be conceived as the purity of an atom, but as restoration to union with others and with the Atman, a restoration which not only breaks down the exclusiveness of mine and thine, but the difference between me and thee, taken as egos.

We shall find this, or something very like this, in many great spirits. It occupies a great deal of Plato's thought. Figures like Thrasymachus and Callicles are his archetypal egoists. Sophistry and rhetoric are to be attacked because they make true communication impossible. Sophistry is not dialogue, because the latter is the coming together of two souls, not the consumption of one by the other. Government must be the therapy which heals torn souls, and not the crushing of the weaker by the stronger. You cannot know yourself except in company, and you cannot have true company where grasping desire sets the tone of human relationships. We are very far indeed from Hobbes, for whom grasping desire and egoism were the very movement of life itself.

The critique of the ego is central in Buddhism. The ego and its grasping desire are the source of the world's misery. But Gautama does not play off the soul against the body as Plato does. Mind is one of the five *skandas*, which constitute a human being, and which deliver him into the hands of change. We are all subject to time and change, and the whole man, insofar as he is constituted by the five *skandas*, will perish. The empirical self has no immortality. There is no Nirvana for the empirical self, which we must play off against the eternal essence, which is not *mine* but transcends all egos and is one with the Atman. We are far from Descartes, for whom each ego is a substance, and for whom a substance is that which "requires nothing beyond itself either to be or to be conceived".

Descartes believed that he could prove the immortality of this thinking substance, and that his philosophy was compatible with the Christian faith. Many of his critics today would say that his thought, like that of Hobbes, really shows its compatibility with the rise of Capitalism. When Hobbes reduces man to a sheer flux of desires, he is constructing a man suitable to consume the products of the machine, which is profitable as long as there is a maximum of desire for its goods, and of men led by the nose by advertisers.

The concern about individual immortality, in the capitalist era of the West, is something very remarkable. It becomes heresy for a Christian to deny it.

In this matter, it is perhaps better to be a Buddhist than that kind of Christian. Gautama told his followers not to waste their time on the question. He held that the desire for individual immortality only showed that grasping desire had not been overcome. It was a phenomenon of egoism. Our empirical selves become so much the object of our own desire that we cannot loosen our grasp. The desire for immortality is an apotheosis of selfishness.

In the West, in our era, private enterprise is the soil in which a craving for individual immortality breeds. The stress on the individual in religion makes for private enterprise in salvation. It is a commercialised Christianity.

This accounts for the relationship between Feuerbach and Marx, because it enables us to understand why Feuerbach wrote a critique of immortality which had a profound effect on Marx's economics. To storm the citadel of Heaven was to attack a fragmented society with its economic cannibalism. Hence Marx came to hold that a critique of religion was necessary as the basis for the economic critique of this vale of tears. Christianity had become a sanctuary for grasping desire.

The association by Buddhism of egoism with grasping desire has its Western counterparts. But the Buddhist emphasis on rooting out grasping desire may persuade us that all desire is bad, which is not the doctrine of the great Western thinkers. "If you want nothing, how are you unhappy?" the old man asks Rasselas, and the prince replies:

> That I want nothing, or that I know not what I want, is the cause of my complaint; if I had any known want, I should have a certain wish; that wish would excite endeavour, and I should not there repine to see the sun move so slowly towards the western mountain, or lament when the day breaks, and sleep will no longer hide me from myself ... But possessing all that I can want; I find one day and one hour exactly like another, except that the latter is still more tedious than the former.

He seems to be in the mood of Hamlet, "How weary, stale, flat and unprofitable seem to me all the uses of this world."

Rasselas has a desire for desire, and it is essential to have a desire. Not all desires are grasping desires. As St

Thomas says, they must be *per conformitatem ad appetitum rectum*, i.e. *de corde pura*.* But to be without any desire is dreadful. Man's life is a life in time. We go from the past into the future, and it is desire which gives our experience the dimensions of a future. To have no desire is to have no future, and this is a dreadful condition. Sometimes, in a mood of depression, or in the dark night, one has no future. In this state one desires no food, no sex and indeed one does not even want to fasten one's shoes: in this state all one wishes for is death, a desire which is the end of time and desire.

To have no desire is one thing; to have all desire satisfied is another. The latter is eternity, the co-existence of desire and its satisfaction: *ubi non praevenit rem desiderium, nec desiderio minus est praemium*.† The absence of desire may be a pathological boredom, the end of time in time, desperation. Hope is the validation of time. Despair is its negation. Surely hell is endless time, meaningless time, time without the consummation of hope. To be hopeless is to have lost faith in time, which is not something which the clock measures, but which our desires measure.

Perhaps the endless time of the universe is the endless desire of God, his vivid life to which we conform in hope.

---

* In conformity with right desire, that is, arising from a clean heart.

† "Where the desire does not precede what satisfies it,
Nor is the heart's possessing less than the heart's desire."
– Abelard.

Therefore place no trust in philosophies which pretend to satisfy our temporal desires. They are promising hell. St Augustine, the philosopher of love and of desire, says that there is implanted in us a desire of something eternal, in the finding of which there is an everlasting happiness. It is always with us. What is eternity? Washing up. That touch of the future, of something *to be* done, contains God, because there is in it some trace of his eternal desire.

As we grow older, some deep desires and enthusiasms fail. We no longer wish to climb the impossible rock face, run the record mile, or catch the biggest fish. Some old friendships weaken, some old loves fade. There are crises in life. There are cessations of desire; and we fear old age and death as meaning such cessations. But what we need is the transformation of desire, the discovery of what gave significance to our old loves, the core of the eternal in the temporal.

I have no formula for this discovery, no mathematical certainty that it is not an illusion. But it seems to me implicit in every project to wash up dishes, to light a pipe, or to write a piece like this. These things all look to the future, and things which look to the future contain a germ of glory which only God can release. The act of release is grace and no man can effect it. Man's part is to endure, to make out through just the next five minutes of his own suffering. Even that is a homage to the future which we hope that God will validate. Kim's lama was searching for a river, and he finds it at home, the little river below the mango tope. We hope for a river of healing, but it is hope which becomes the river that heals. Tomorrow is God himself, however awful tomorrow may look to me.

We find in Western thought rather a dialectic of love and desire than an endeavour to extirpate them. St Augustine in *The City of God* castigates the Stoics for their enmity to the emotions. He calls their attitude to the emotions a hardness which is worse than sin. Plato points out that philo-sophia is a love affair, a love affair for which the community exists.

We must not be misled by the simplifications which Plato uses in the *Republic*, book II, where he speaks about the origin and growth of the state. People come together, he says, because they have basic needs for, for instance, food, clothing and shelter, which they find they can best procure collectively. One may get the impression that he sees men as atomic units of desire, whose desires are pre-collective, and that the state has fulfilled its function when these pre-collective desires are satisfied.

We must remember that Plato is using here a simple diagram, and saw clearly enough that our desires are post-social. The community exists not only to satisfy desires but to create them, and perhaps the latter is its chief function. Of course, there are tares among the wheat, as Plato indicates in his description of the state which has inflammation, but it is also there that our desires grow in a social context until their *raison d'être* in the love of wisdom, in the perfect community, is seen.

As our desires are refined, they seek a community, an everlasting city, which can never be fully realised on earth.

The purpose of the city is to propel us towards a heavenly city which can never be fully realised in history. We come to long for an immortal city, so that the division of labour looks not merely at the provision of houses and shoes but to the glory of the forms. There, then, is the ladder of love, described in the *Symposium*, by which we climb to the vision of the Beautiful, which is the culmination of our desire and search for the whole. It is true that his is a progressive escape from craving desire, but not an escape from desire.

This is very true indeed for the teaching of St Augustine. *Nemo est qui non amet*,* and he would not and could not have it otherwise. That is why he is the Doctor Caritatis. What we have in the *Confessions* is a *scala amoris*, a ladder of love, where St Augustine reaches enlightenment by climbing up the mound of his dead loves. It is indicative of the wideness of his sympathies that, while all evil arises from misplaced or perverted love, he holds it to be true that at the heart of every desire, no matter how perverse or inordinate, there is a spark of the divine love which can be freed from its trappings. Even sin is a sort of love in which the hand of the Creator can be seen, and which can be disentangled from grasping desire to become an obedience to God, and a reception of his love.

St Augustine holds that there are two kinds of *amor sui*, or self-love, a good and an evil. There is an *amor sui*

---

*   Love is everybody's destiny.

which is a norm for the love of others, whom we are commanded to love as we love ourselves. We are to love ourselves as created images of God so that our *amor sui* is an *amor Dei*, so that our self-love is God-love. We are then able to see and love in our neighbour the image of God in him. The evil love of ourselves is what St Augustine calls the *amor concupiscentiae*. This is the grasping desire, the egoism which creates the earthly city. It is an encapsulation, which is also an idolatry of the self, grasping itself feverishly, instead of relaxing to God. It is the fruit of pride which refers everything to our own egos as though they were the highest of beings. This is to work perdition to both ourselves and our world; an egoism which sets up the devil's kingdom. What sets up the City of God is a love for our own nature precisely as creature, and the love of God as fulfilling all desire.

Therefore, in his commentary on St John, St Augustine quotes with approval the words of Virgil, *trahit sua quemque voluptas*, commenting that it is a man's desire which draws him on, not necessity but desire, not obligation but delight. Give me a man, says he, who loves, give me a man who gasps for the fountain of eternal life (Kim's lama's river) and he will know what I am talking about. The emotionless man (*frigidus*) won't.

Both Eastern and Western contemplative thought have made a distinction between the "I" and the real self. The separative self feels lonely, isolated and threatened. Descartes's thinking mind is cut off from sensible nature and from other selves. Hobbes's natural man is a threatened, fearful atom; his mind is calculative for its own self-interest. We are all putting up a front to assist us in our own aggrandisement, building up a facade which is conventional and artificial. The worth of a man "consisteth in comparison". This comparison is in terms of power, wealth, reputation, useful friendships. This facade is a mask and we can all say with Descartes, *larvatus prodeo*, "I go forth masked." It is by virtue of the mask that we can join in the rat race with its fear of insecurity, its construction of a legal system which will secure our "rights", the desertion of a man when he's down. Social intercourse is a matter of wearing the right mask and manoeuvring it gainfully. The use of reason is to subtend this. We become the objects of our own thought, and lose our true subjectivity.

This is not a knowing of oneself. It is the obliteration of our real selves, and the proper knowing of oneself is to let the real self, which includes the body and the emotions and the subconscious, speak. It is largely a matter of letting go, and is worst served by digging anxiously into our interiors. We must lie back relaxedly and listen.

Good writing, for instance, is writing from the centre, something done through me rather than by me. If a writer is not listening as well as talking, he will fail to communicate. Indian thought distinguishes between the self and the Self; the Taoists between wisdom and discursive thinking. Wisdom is a surrender to the Tao, where our natural endowment comes to its rights. Lao-tzu tells us that we are wiser than we know, a statement which gives their dues to the body and the subconscious. What we require to be enlightened is a sort of stupidity. Again there is a contrast with Descartes and his clear and distinct ideas which are to be methodically used by a mind disconnected from the body, in order to make ourselves the masters and possessors of nature.

The Zen masters, on the other hand, tell us that Zen is our ordinary mind, that it is eating when we are hungry, and drinking when we are thirsty; and that, instead of trying like Descartes to abolish death by a methodical science of medicine, we should realise that whatever age we are is the right age for us to be, and that we are likely to live longer by resignation to the Tao than by an anxious effort to prolong our lives by technics. Descartes transposes eternity to duration, and wishes to secure the duration of his body in order that he, and he alone, will be able to perfect the new sciences, which, as Maritain so well insisted, crowd wisdom out.

The self, which excludes others, and the Self, which is found in the practice of the presence of God, and which is a return to what we are by nature, a gift of Ourselves to ourselves, occupy different times. The time of the ego has a different past, present, and future from that of the Self. The ego drives us to fugues into the past and the future. In its preoccupation with the past it cherishes thoughts of such things as revenge, especially against those who have injured its self-esteem. It suffers remorse, something quite different from repentance, which redeems time, whereas remorse is a spiritual sickness. It lives in anxiety about the future: How will I die? Have I enough property to secure my old age? Will my country be invaded in war? These are all questions which affect our stance in the present.

The ego is closely tied up with ownership and with grasping desire, which is concerned with the future rather than with the present. We are alarmed at the prospect of losing what we possess, we speculate on how to increase our property, we are always trying to *insure*. We are anxious about our status and our power. Perhaps the best analysis of the fearful self and its property will be found in the *Leviathan*, where Hobbes measures the *worth* of a man by his property and the power which it gives him. Stirner's *The Ego and Its Own* helps us considerably in understanding the time of selfishness.

The Self which the ego obscures, however, does not try to gain possession of the whole world, because it already possesses it, not as an exclusive individual, but as a social being, that is, as a being which has no being except as an image of the One, or, if you like, is founded in the Atman.

The separative self, to the degree in which it asserts itself, is nothing. It has ceased to be image. St Augustine, when dealing with the doctrine of the resemblance of all things to the Trinity and their participation in the life of the Trinity by resemblance, tells us to remember that that participation is by resemblance only. Christian doctrine does not hold that created things emanate from God. It does not hold that creation diminishes the substance of God, or that created things are part of the divine substance. We have to do with a doctrine of creation out of nothing.

That is the privilege of omnipotence.

There is a sense, then, in which creatures are nothing. Their being is simply to be *as image*. Through them the divine love returns to itself with no other motive than the generosity of omnipotent love. Creatures of themselves have nothing. Therefore, if we speak of the creature as participating in the divine nature, we do not mean that it is part of the divine nature. Compared with God it is entirely insubstantial. It has no meaning except the accent by which it is spoken by the divine Logos. We come to the paradoxical conclusion that it is itself because it is nothing. That is why, for St Augustine, the archetypal sin of spirits is to claim to be something *in their own right*. All that the creature has a right to love is the love of God in him and in creatures, because they *are* nothing else.

The self has no being other than that being which is given it by a gratuitous Love. Its activity is, as it were, a translation into time of that love. Hence the phrase that time is the moving image of eternity. For rational beings a right disposition is to will to unite the image to the original. It is in this union that creaturely being fulfils its meaning.

In Buddhism, the return to the Self is a not dissimilar pilgrimage. Nirvana is *not* total extinction but rather the extinction of the grasping ego. It is the latter which is the creator of nothingness, or rather, a relapse into it. As St Thomas says,

> God loves sinners in so far as they are existing natures, for they have existence and have it from Him. In

> so far as they are sinners, they have no existence at all,
> but fall short of it; and this in them is not from God.

The Buddhist would say that the grasping ego is caught in the Karmic time of *samsara*.

But if we have to step outside of the time of the separative self, where do we take our stance? We notice that the egoistic man is always destroying the present, which he poisons by his anxiety about the future or his regrets about the past. But the present is the only reality, so that we can say that the egoist lives in an unreal world. But the true self finds itself in the present, eating when he is hungry and having no care for the morrow, and knowing that every day is the best day of his life.

Both Eastern and Western spirits have maintained that the secret of life is to live in the present. This is not something to be strained after, because then we shall have sold the present to the future, to the *then* in which we hope to enjoy the present. Asceticism and other disciplines cannot bring this about, which is why Gautama chose the "middle way". But "to live in the present" is a saying which is easily misunderstood. We cannot not have a past and a future, because we are human beings who have to act, that is, to constitute a future, guided by what we learnt in the past.

If I am to drink when I am thirsty I must have found out what water is, and look forward to a body which is replenished. When Christ tells us to have no care for the morrow he is not telling us to be drop-outs, or not to plough and sow, but not to save up today's manna for tomorrow. He admonishes us not to be *anxious* about tomorrow, or hag-ridden about the past. He is not telling us to take a sledgehammer to the deep freeze, but to relax into this day. Even if it is a day of sorrow we can meet it only by relaxing into the sorrow. The present hour is most like God's eternity because it is that in which things *are*. We should treat each day as the kiss of God upon the universe, or the sharing of his joy that it is good. We cannot dispense with ego-consciousness, but we can avoid identifying it with what we are. It is simply the top of the iceberg, supported by something which it cannot reach by taking thought.

But for those who think that wisdom comes only from the East, I shall quote Emerson:

> Write it on your heart that every day is the best day in the year. No man has learned anything rightly, until he knows that every day is Doomsday. 'Tis the old secret of the Gods that they come in low disguises. 'Tis the vulgar great who come dizened with gold and jewels. Real kings hide away their crowns in their wardrobes, and affect a plain and poor exterior. In the Norse legend of our ancestors, Odin dwells in a fisher's hut, and patches a boat. In the Hindoo legends, Hari dwells a peasant among peasants. In the Greek legend, Apollo lodges with the shepherds of Admetus; and Jove liked to rusticate among the poor Ethiopians. So, in our history, Jesus is born in a barn and his twelve peers are fishermen ... We owe to genius always the same debt,

> of lifting the curtain from the common, and showing us that divinities are sitting disguised in the seeming gang of gipsies and pedlars. In daily life what distinguishes the master is the using of those materials he has, instead of looking about for what are more renowned, or what others have used well ... Do not refuse the employment which the hour gives you, for one more ambitious ... The use of history is to give value to the present hour and its duty. That is good which commends to me my country, my climate, my means and materials, my associates. I knew a man in a certain religious exaltation, who 'thought it an honour to wash his own face'. He seemed to me more sane than those who hold themselves cheap.

It is the common which is divine. That is why the true poetic imagination is not a flight into some airy realm, but an insight into the "isness" of what is here and now, for every creature is an incarnation. What is the Buddha? The dog on the mat. He prayeth best who loveth best all creatures great or small. Homage to a brickbat is not idolatry but its opposite. We may so far forget ourselves that we go out into the brick, and then a poem is born. All good poems are poems about the isness of things. That is why *haiku* poems are great poetry. The separative ego cannot write poetry, because poetry is incarnation.

The first Incarnation is the creation of the world by God. He is present all about us in this transient garb which is the world. Hence Zen recommends living like a ball on a mountain stream, and eating when you are hungry and drinking when you are thirsty, which comes to much the same, as is said in *The Cloud of Unknowing*:

> You will ask me perhaps, how you are to control yourself with due care in the matter of food and drink and sleep and so on. My answer is brief: 'Take what comes!' Do this thing without ceasing and without care day by day, and you will know well enough, with a real discretion, when to begin and when to stop in everything else. I cannot believe that a soul who goes on in this work with complete abandon, day and night, will make mistakes in mundane matters. If he does, he is, I think, the type who will always get things wrong.

2 : The Ego in Indian Thought

What the Buddha announced was the cause and the cure of suffering. Now the cause of suffering is the obtrusion and magnification of the ego: the suffering life is the egocentric. What Buddhists mean by ego is what Christians mean by pride, which is the idolatry of the self.

We must remember that Buddhism rises out of Hinduism, and retains much of the *Upanishad* teaching. Now at the centre of the latter is the doctrine that Atman is Brahman, and that Atman is the soul or self of all things. It is the soul or Self of ourselves too. It is the Self of our own self, and the realisation of this, not intellectually but in a concrete experience, is the end of suffering. Ego, or the small self, must be supplanted by the great Self, or Atman. That is what is meant by the famous statement: That art thou. As St Paul says, we must put off the old man, the ego tattered by sin and ignorance, and enter into the joy of our Lord. Union with Atman brings what is real in ourselves to fruition.

Both Buddhism and Christianity hold to this idea of the real in ourselves. We can, however, obscure it. What in essence we are is the image of God. Buddhism declares that the real self is Brahman, that is, that we are to look for God in ourselves. In this there is nothing repugnant to Christianity. There has long been a tradition in the Christian Church which has insisted that the way to God was inwards, until we find Him who, as St Augustine said, is nearer to us than ourselves. This union with God in the depths of the soul, this restoration of the image to the original, is not the final triumph of pride but the obliteration of ego, so that God may be all in all.

As far as Buddhism is concerned, this real self is not something to be constructed by us. It is not a real self of the future to be built up by us. Indeed, the latter would be an entirely frustrating effort since we should have to build up this ideal on the basis of what at present we are. It would merely be a projection of ego which will bind us more firmly than ever. We are already what we must be, and we must let be rather than fall into the trap of idealism. We have, rather, to remove the rubble to find the treasure underneath. What we are is something to be revealed and not made. The ideal self is a Procrustes bed in which the reality will be smothered. We are in the hands of what we are, of the Self which ego tries to obliterate.

Buddhism aims at the destruction of the ego, a destruction so thoroughgoing that it may at first stagger the Westerner. But, the reduction of the ego to an impermanent flux which we cannot hold on to is central in the Buddhist therapy. There is no substantial enduring self. Neither is there a mind which is less transient than the body. All are impermanent: bodies, sensations, perceptions, impressions of past deeds and thoughts (*sankharas*), and consciousness itself. All these are not Self but sorrow. To be rid of them is not to be reduced to nothing but to find reality. Even immortality is an illusion for the Buddhist insofar as this belief is simply a refusal of the ego to let loose of itself, as itself an object of grasping desire.

We have to be careful here in our interpretations. A pantheist interpretation is possible for which the self will lose its sense of identity and be lost like a drop of water in the ocean of being. This is repugnant to the Western sense of the importance of the person, which rests on religious grounds. As Sri Ramakrishna put it: to want to suck sugar is not to want to be sugar. If we hold that God is unique, and that He made all things in His image, then that uniqueness must also be imaged, as a permanent value for eternity. One cannot become God because one is not God. What there will be is the joy of the creature in the presence of God.

One finds this way of thinking also in Hinduism. Ramanuja's Absolute is a personal God.

> When the freed self sees God face to face, its logical outlook (rational conclusions) becomes a spiritual insight, and freed from the nescience of the empirical life, it expands into omniscience. It has a sense of the infinite and sees everything with the eye of the all-self. When the self is Brahmanised, it is stripped of its selfhood and sense of separateness ... The infinite remains, but the fetters of finitude and individualism are removed.
> (SWAMI PRABHAVANANDA, THE SPIRITUAL HERITAGE OF INDIA, PP. 312–13)

This also appears in Sri Ramakrishna, who said:

> There are two kinds of ego – one ripe, and the other unripe. The unripe ego thinks, 'This is my house, my son, my this, my that.' The ripe ego thinks, 'I am the servant of the Lord, I am his child; I am the Atman, immortal, free; I am Pure Consciousness.'
> (QUOTED BY PRABHAVANANDA, P. 352)

This is the language not of absorption by but devotion to and union with a person. This agrees well enough with the position of Ramanuja, that there is never a dissolution of *jiva*hood, or individual personality, even in liberation after death.

But ego, the small and separate self, is, for Hindu and Buddhist spirituality, the enemy to be overcome. Thus Patanjali says:

> To regard the non-eternal as eternal, the impure as pure, the painful as pleasant, and the non-Self as the Purusa – this is ignorance. (YOGA SUTRAS II.5)

In Christian language to regard the ego as God is pride or ignorance.

> The obstacles to enlightenment – the causes of man's sufferings – are ignorance, egoism, attachment, aversion, and the desire to cling to life. (II.3)

It will be profitable to look at Patanjali's account of the genesis of these obstacles. The core of the matter, we are to observe, is distinguishing mind from Atman, Purusa, or Spirit. Patanjali holds that mind is made up of three components, *manas*, *buddhi*, and *ahamkāra*. By *manas* is meant the recording faculty, that which registers sense-impressions of the outside world. *Buddhi* classifies these impressions and reacts to them, e.g. such and such impressions are pleasant, and therefore sought. *Ahamkāra* is the ego-sense, which claims these impressions as its own – *I* am seeing white or *I* am feeling pleasure – and stores them up as *my* knowledge.

The mind seems to be intelligent and conscious. Yoga philosophy makes the shattering statement that it is not. The mind has only a borrowed or secondary intelligence. The primary intelligence is *Purusa*, pure consciousness, the Great Self. The mind dresses itself up in that consciousness and masquerades as conscious. Knowledge or perception is a thought wave in the mind, and all knowledge is thus objective. Even introspection and self-knowledge through observation is objective knowledge.

The mind, thus, is not the seer, but an object or instrument of knowledge, an object like objects in the outside world. The Purusa, the real subject or consciousness, remains unknown. But the mind claims to be the Purusa, it claims to be God, and that is what the ego is: a parody of divinity for which we claim a prime reality. All sin and suffering have their origin here.

When something in the external world strikes the senses the ego-sense identifies with this impression. If it is a pleasant impression, we feel, *I* am happy; if an impression of red, *I* am seeing red.

This false identification is the cause of all our misery;

even the ego's temporary sensation of happiness brings anxiety, a fear that the object of pleasure will be taken away ... The *Purusa*, in contrast, remains forever outside the power of thought waves ... It follows, therefore, that man can never know his real Self as long as *Purusa* is identified with the products of mind.
(PRABHAVANANDA, PP. 233–4)

We have constructed a solid subject for experience by an act of mistaken identity, and laid all our bets on it.

One of the sources of this analysis is a passage in the *Kena Upanishad* (1.1–2):

At whose behest does the mind think? Who bids the body live? Who makes the tongue speak? Who is that effulgent Being that directs the eye to form and colour and the ear to sound? The Atman is the ear of the ear, mind of the mind, speech of the speech. He is also breath of the breath and eye of the eye. Having given up the false identification of the Atman with the senses and the mind, and knowing the Atman to be Brahman, the wise become immortal.

We may set up this enlightenment, this consummation, as an ideal, but while it is still *I* who meditate on *my* ideal, I am still frustrated and will remain so until I realise that the real I *is* the ideal, not something of the future, but *now*. What a world of selfishness can be concealed in *my Ideal*!

Another way of saying this – we are still with Patanjali – is that the Self has been enmeshed in the activities of the psychic nature, meaning the three components of the mind. We are caught in sense and imagination. This seems to be all that we are – as Hobbes was to affirm – and then our lives will be solitary, poor, nasty, brutish and short. We are the slaves of pleasure and vain curiosity. It follows that these psychic activities must be controlled. They are not in themselves evil, but are spiritual powers which have fallen. They must be released and restored, which will happen when we uncover the immortal in us, not by violent struggle but by quietly letting the Purusa be. A guru like Marpa lived outwardly a very ordinary life as a householder.

> Man has a sense of self which seems to him to be continuous and solid. When a thought or emotion or event occurs, there is a sense of someone being conscious of what is happening. You sense that *you* are [hearing] these words. This sense of self is actually a transitory, discontinuous event, which in our confusion seems to be quite solid and continuous. Since we take our confused view as being real, we struggle to maintain and enhance this solid self. We try to feed it pleasures and shield it from pain.

This unripe self is what is called the samsaric self, the self of birth and death. To it corresponds the samsaric world, a world which we try to make more real by solidifying it by means of concepts and laws, which try to stop the sheer flow of experience. Thus we take "cat" to be a form in the Platonic sense, a pattern which endures and outlives the transient cats of our experience. Or again we "discover" laws of nature which state timeless connections between events.

It is central to Buddhist thought to hold that the phenomenal or samsaric world, the world of sense-experience, is correlative with the ego. The world, they say, is what we make it, and this is an anthropomorphic world upon which we project the mistakes we make about ourselves. It arises from the subject-object dichotomy, which is overcome only by the insight: *that art thou*. What we meet in the world is what we put there. Thus enmity or misfortune is something which we do rather than suffer. Every mind constructs its world, and as the mind, so the world. It is we who set up the oppositions which frighten us. We are the source of our own fears to which we lend solidity and an objective basis.

Emancipation from a tyrannical world occurs when we realise that this world is only phenomenal, that is, apparent. To reach reality is to transcend it, and to arrive at the union of all things in the Atman. The soul in things is then seen to be my soul, and reality to be non-dual. That is what is meant by saying that every nature is a Buddha nature.

This doctrine plays a central part in *The Tibetan Book of the Dead*, which maintains that all conditions or realms of samsaric existence, heavens, hells, worlds, are purely phenomenal, mists dissolved by the sun of reality. All phenomena are illusory and transient, and seem real only to ego. There are really no such beings as gods, or demons, or spirits or suchlike creatures. These are phenomena dependent on a cause, and this cause is the griping desire of the ego. The shapes of horror which we may encounter after death are objectifications of what is in us, and disappear with knowledge of the true self. The realisation, *that art thou*, dissolves all demons, and by it we are rescued from hell and rebirth.

Union with God, and being your true Self, are one and the same. This is Nirvana, the end of all suffering, which we shed with ego and its ignorance. This union is prayer and praise. Petitionary prayer belongs to the subject-object dichotomy, for it arises from a desire for something. This is a teaching of all higher religion. Thus St James says (4.1–3):

> Where do these wars and battles between yourselves first start? Isn't it precisely in the desires fighting inside your own selves? You want something and you have not got it; so you are prepared to kill. You have an ambition that you cannot satisfy; so you fight to get your way by force. Why you don't have what you want is because you don't pray for it; when you do pray and don't get it, it is because you have not prayed properly, you have prayed for something to indulge your own desires.

The ego can neither pray nor create. It throws up illusions which are real only to its own distempered state. Prayer and poetry reveal reality. They do not create fantasies.

We may say, then, that the aim of the Buddhist ascesis

is humility. Ascesis is not struggling or straining but relaxing into what we are, relaxing into the egoless Self in both humility and freedom. In meditation one does not strive to have thoughts, but to let their presence or absence simply roll over one. It is in the gaps between them that one may discern the Self.

Ego cannot pray because humility *is* a prayer. Creation is a prayer, and to pray is to be created. "Send forth thy spirit and we shall be created." But to receive this creation we must be willing to accept the darkness of Chaos and sink into the Void, which reveals itself not to be nothing but everything. The Buddhist Nirvana is not annihilation but the ascent out of the dark waters where desire has been washed away. Bliss is not getting what we want, but being what we are.

I conclude with a question to which I do not have a clear answer. Have we to write off the variety and the beauties of the perceived world as samsaric? I think that Platonism can save the appearances, since it could not otherwise have inspired poets, who have to do with the particular and concrete. To say, the corn was orient and immortal wheat, is not to sponge out corn. It is ignorance of the oneness of things which constitutes the samsaric world, but oneness need not blot out differentiation. There is such a thing as unity in and through difference.

To see God in a stone is to make the stone more and not less stony. Philosophers in the Biblical tradition have been able to maintain this by virtue of the doctrine of Creation, by which a unique God creates in his image beings each one of which is as image unique. That no two leaves are the same could be seen by a Hopkins as a glory. "Christ plays in ten thousand places," and illuminates what the Chinese would call "the ten thousand things". It is uniqueness which makes things relevant to each other, and enables one to contribute to the other.

We desire the being of others, but this is a generous and not a grasping desire, and this generous desire operates at all levels of the universe. It requires a de Sade to see the universe as an area of mutual cannibalism. And certainly one's involvement in such a universe would not be overcome by finding a One which swallows all the oysters. It is the diabolic desire which consumes because it cannot create. There is a Carpenter who does not swallow. Kingfishers catch fire when they dart into the Void.

We must certainly not rush to the conclusion that the Void is the absolutely negative. Thus the Hassidic philosophy holds that

> creating is to be created: the divine moves and overcomes us. And to be created is ecstasy: only one who sinks into the Nothing of the unconditioned receives the forming hand of the spirit.
> (BUBER, *THE LEGEND OF THE BAAL SHEM*)

What arises from this immersion in the void is not samsaric, and what arises must be unique as a poem is unique which never can be written twice. Hence Martin Buber can write:

> Uniqueness is the essential good of man that is given to him to unfold. And just this is the meaning of the

return [rebirth], that his uniqueness may become ever purer, and more complete; and that in each new life the one who has returned may stand in ever more untroubled and undistributed incomparability. For pure uniqueness and pure perfection are one, and he who has become so entirely individual that no otherness any longer has any power over him or place in him has completed the journey and is redeemed and rests in God.

This seems to me to be a very good characterisation of the cessation of rebirth, and of Nirvana. It is uniqueness which makes us both munificent and eternally secure. The Boddhisatva is compassionate because he is eternally secure. That security is the end of sorrow. We have emerged from the Dark Waters to drink the Water which takes away all thirst.

"You never enjoy the world aright," said Thomas Traherne, "till the sea itself floweth in your veins, till you are clothed with the heavens, and crowned with the stars: and perceive yourself to be the sole heir of the whole world, and more than so, because men are in it who are everyone sole heirs as well as you."

That seems to me the real meaning of *tat tvam asi*, thou art that.

3 : The Importance of Being Human

Philosophy ought to start with anthropology in the Continental use of the term. What comes first is not theory of knowledge, but the problem of the being of man. We shall appreciate this better the more clearly we see how anthropomorphic all our knowledge is. I think that I first came to see this when considering Aquinas's opinions on angelic knowledge.

When we realise what angels are, his argument goes, we realise that their knowledge must be very different from ours. Since they are incorporeal, their knowledge cannot, like ours, commence through the senses. Only metaphorically can we say that they see the world. We can have some knowledge by analogy of angelic knowledge according as we know something of their being; and their knowledge is angelomorphic and in relation to their mode of being. Given that each angel constitutes a species, we are led to contemplate a vast hierarchy of knowledges, each true of the same object which is constituted in its integrity by the creative knowledge of God. The God's-eye view of a thing is what constitutes it to be what it is, and the knowledge of lower beings is proportioned and measured by God's creative act.

Once we seize the possibility of a scaled multiplicity of knowledges, and of an absolute divine knowledge, we can relativise our own. It is the knowledge of an embodied spirit constituted to be what it is by the fact that it commences with, and terminates in, sense experience. It spiritualises matter because it is the knowledge of an embodied being, a body made of matter but different from other material things by being the way of being of a spiritual nature.

We are at present more likely to look to the animals than to the angels; to ask: What is this room to my dog? What is the world cynomorphically considered? What sort of world does an acute sense of smell give you? In what sense does the dog live in the "same" world as I? Partly, no doubt, we constitute the same world by co-operation, but it must be an identity through difference. The important thing to see is that if there can be a dog's-eye view of the world, there can also be a cabbage-eye view of it. Cabbages too have their sense organs.

Man's knowledge is relative to what he is, that is, he lives in an anthropomorphic world, which is constructed according to the kind of body which he has. Thus he sees the world as ordered coloured shapes, because he has the kind of eye and hand which he has. It is the use of the hand which gives him left and right, up and down, small and big. He estimates the spaces round him by the fact that he is, say, six feet tall, their penetrability by the fact that he can walk. Space comes to mean something different for him according as he makes new artefacts, e.g. Mars rockets. His physics is *man's* physics, not a disembodied absolute physics, by virtue of which he calls God a mathematician, and then goes on to call himself God because he himself is a mathematician.

Furthermore, man has a history in time. He has a relation to the world and to other human beings in time, he succeeds and precedes other human beings in time, and indeed the whole sense of before and after, past and future, is a gigantic piece of anthropomorphism. That is why all his knowledge is invaded by death. His body, through which he knows, is a perishable body, and of this he is aware. Man is a being which knows that it shall die. In this he is more privileged – or cursed – than dogs or angels. His whole sense of time is permeated by this knowledge, and the ridiculous shortness of his life. The quality of our lives depends on the quality of our acceptance of death; of our sense of whether our individual life will be long or short; of the genuineness of our perception that this very minute may be the last of our lives, and that we have no time to waste, but only to act well, in which lies the dignity of a mortal being, capable of taking responsibility for his time.

It is this historicity of our knowledge which makes possible a sociology of knowledge. Our knowledge is a knowledge of man *in via*, evolving a way which he travels with other men, so that his anthropomorphism is that of the body politic, and not only of his own. The human world is a collective world, and is spoken by a language common to a group. The world is my world because it is a human world, built up co-operatively in historical time. Truth is relative to history, angelic truth to *aevum*, God's truth to *aeternitas*, in which alone there is no relativity. *Quod Deus est, quod Deus est aeternus, quod Deus est sua aeternitas*, are words of Aquinas which climb upwards like the strokes of a great gong. Human importance or unimportance is constituted by our relation to death and eternity. Ripeness is all, and the condition for it is the sloughing off of self-importance. What is man that thou art mindful of him? His estimation of himself will also be anthropomorphic and, unless it is identical to his humility, it will be far from truth.

If we cannot ascribe an absolute value to man, he does, however, possess the capacity to ask questions about his own importance. He may ascribe divinity to himself, or he may degrade himself to dust and stones, or he may strike a mean and call himself dust inspired by God. His self-valuations vary, a fact which ought to persuade him to a decent humility. There is a pseudo-humility, however, which it were well to avoid. A being which can proclaim its own insignificance can hardly be insignificant, and it will be instructive to look at one of these claims to insignificance, a claim which inspires the lyrical melancholy of Russell's free man's worship. It arises from our obsession with the quantitative, and reveals the nemesis of the clear and distinct idea of quantity, and the real distinction of mind and body, which, as Descartes drew it, was an objective distinction: We are not looking at one through the other; we are looking at both. Hence the human body is assimilated to all other bodies animate or inanimate and compared to them by means of a common measure.

A common way of asserting the insignificance of man is to regard him quantitatively: a couple of cubic feet of flesh, a handful of minerals, subject to fate and chance, and to play this off against the vast stellar spaces. Insignificant may mean small, or, alternatively, without meaning. The latter affirmation can be made only by a being who has meaning, or knows what it is, and then proceeds to negate it. The meaning of life then becomes meaninglessness, a suicidal situation, for "meaningless" is an evaluation possible only to a being who experiences meaning, or apprehends his being and meaning as one.

This is a very common fault because we are surrounded by science and its technological products, and this gives rise to the habit of treating everything as an object. This is what science does and ought to do, because it is only by distancing itself from what it investigates that it can give a true account of it. The individual subjectivity of the scientist must be bracketed because the investigator wants to achieve propositions which mean the same to all subjects, subjects whom he regards as investigating objects, themselves capable of being investigated. The scientist takes a stand outside the object in relation to which he is an absent presence, absent because he wishes to keep the object pure, present because he wants to know and deal with the object, and to relate to it with his techniques. But this is a condition of alienation both from himself and from the world.

At the centre of this alienation lies the inner split between oneself as object and as subject. We think of ourselves as objects, but objects don't think or evaluate themselves. Looked at from the object point of view the body-mind relation is in principle, and absolutely, insoluble. If I say that I am only a measurable body I should be talking nonsense because what was only body could not think this thought. Mind is a capacity for interiorising the world and ourselves. We can put a man on the moon only because the moon is already in the man. In a sense, a stone has no inside. Only in a very small degree can it register the world.

We say that we *have* a body, we *have* a mind, as we *have* a chisel or a saw. This leads to an instrumental notion of body or mind. When Hume says that reason is and ought to be the slave of the desires, he is proposing an instrumental view of the mind. But if the mind is something that we *use* to gain some higher end, what is that end, and who is it that wields the instrument? What is its possessor? What uses the spirit as if it were its owner? It is much more likely to be something sub-rational rather than super-rational, that is, the mind may become the instrument of darkness, and such a use may be in the end diabolical. In fact it will be, if reason is not tempered by wisdom.

When Descartes transmutes the spirit into reason or mind, there are no longer any degrees of knowledge.*

---

* "There is no small irony in the fact that what is the fundamental illusion for Buddhist experience is taken as the fundamental axiom of Cartesian thought." (M. Conrad Hyers, *Zen and the Comic Spirit*, p. 199)

There is nothing but the instrumental use of science to make us "the masters and possessors of nature". What lies behind the reason would then appear to be a master, perhaps the naked will to power, or perhaps mere impulse. Plato knew this when he attacked the Sophists, and that is why he saw intelligence as the essence of man and not his instrument. A man should not use himself but be himself, and if this is so, then Hume defects from humanity. He who uses himself must expect to be used by others.

The idolatry of science arose from its being regarded as a tool which we could use for any and every purpose, or from which there could be no appeal. At the end of the nineteenth century Sherlock Holmes and Dr Thorndyke appear as culture heroes, and remain very attractive period pieces. Sherlock is sheer logical brain. When his brain is out of employment, there is nothing in him in which he can rest, and so he resorts to cocaine. He had to be a bachelor so as to eviscerate himself more completely. Dr Thorndyke collects facts *ad nauseam* and represents a society which made an idol of facts. The sheer power of ratiocination dominates man, and the other elements in his nature, whether higher or lower, starve. To many there were no other elements until the havoc caused by their neglect evoked a Freud and a Jung to bring them to our view. Sherlock Holmes sitting on a pile of cushions smoking shag might solve a problem but he could not penetrate a mystery, though he does have glorious lapses which make him a person. He concludes from a moss rose to God, though this, too, is a rational process.

If then, we *have* a body, it is a Cartesian body, really distinct from mind. The body which we *have* is an opaque, three-dimensional object which we can scientifically investigate. I can see it, prod it, dissect it. In this attitude we miss the great and simple insight that the body appears to us to be opaque precisely because it isn't. It seems opaque because we look at it from the outside as we would look at a chair or a tree. It becomes the investigable self. But this self is not the investigating self. When we look at the self from the outside it becomes opaque. When we shift our point of view, we find that our bodies are really transparencies. As I sit in this room I see furniture, books, my hand. My mind is then a mirror just registering what is there, and putting it there. "Here" is the convergence of things at a point which is penetrable to them or through whose transparency they can enter.

Our bodies look opaque because we perceive through them, because they are transparent, registering what is there with absolute immediacy. They offer no barrier to the world's presenting itself. Our bodies are a lying open to the world. When we describe, for instance, the optic nerves as an explanation of visual sensation, we are performing a secondary action, talking about the eye seen and not the eye seeing. We may perform the curious action of saying that we can't know objects as they are because they are mediated to us by a complex physical apparatus, but which, were it not veridically seen, would not explain anything. I *am* the presence of the world by virtue of my transparency. When Descartes cuts us off from the world there is no longer any I. *Cogito, ergo sum* makes objective science possible but turns the I into an it.

Sense data stream into us, and we go out to them because of our transparency. That is the first act in knowing. *Primum in intellectu cadit ens*. To try to describe the mind in terms only of bodily functions is absurd, because our knowledge of bodily functions is secondary. That is why materialism is absurd: it is second sight and not first sight. We are lanterns because we can call a world into being out of darkness, and we are part of this world. But the embodied ego which we find there obscures the more primary act by which we call this world into being.

It is transparency which precedes opacity, and in a sense creates opacity. The destructive egoisms of man arise from the secondary self and the secondary world which have lost sight of the primal Self. The aim of, for instance, Buddhist meditation is to rest in this primary. If we live only by the transitory secondary ego we are cut off from the primal Self and construct a world of unrealities, including an ego which *has* rather than *is*, and we exist only to have. We have to turn ourselves outside-in if we are not to be destroyed by the thought and material products of the objective attitude.

To say that "I am my body" is materialism only when it is said at the level of secondary ratiocination and not of primary intuition. It is the spirituality of Descartes which is materialistic. One must rather say that mind and spirit are the body as seen from within, in the primary act of constituting the world. The egoless mind and transparent body are one, and for this innocent eye the *maya* of the technological nightmare disappears. This is the loss of the self which finds the Self.

All the trouble arises because we do not distinguish between the body which perceives and the body which we perceive. One of the most flagrant examples is that of Thomas Hobbes, for whom man is only a perceived body, and for whom, since bodies are mutually exclusive, men are mutually exclusive, so that the life of each is selfish and greedy for things desired.

The self which is perceived can never catch up with the self which perceives. The former can be touched and weighed. Of the latter we cannot have that kind of knowledge. We cannot have the clear and certain knowledge at which the measuring mind aims. A civilisation which aims only at measuring the self will be controlled by superficial, i.e. opaque, selves only, selves deprived of inner vision, and which will be crushed by the weight of the *artificialia* with which they seek to satisfy their desires.

By the desire for the real self we live in a common world, a concreated world, free of grasping desire, a world very different from our own, and for which no blueprint is possible because it will surprise us every day. Outer vision makes no sense when divorced from inner vision, and there will be no technological heaven. The latter is only Manichaeanism stood on its head. It is by concentrating on the perceived self that we make a body-soul dichotomy. It is the perceiving self, the inwardness of the body, which constitutes a person capable of resurrection.

What is of more importance than the physical smallness of man is his uniqueness, and this uniqueness extends to the smallest organic being. When considering the vast stellar spaces, I cannot see our planet as a mere transient and fortuitous exception. There may be other life-bearing planets but we cannot expect animate beings on them to be similar to those on our own planet. There may be beings as intelligent or more intelligent than ourselves, but their bodies and minds would be very different. If there are animals and insects and plants we have no reason to suppose that they would be like ours. No two leaves on our own planet are identical. This "insignificant" blown autumn leaf is not only different from all of these other leaves here, but could not possibly be duplicated in all these vast galaxies. It has unspeakably great value, a value as great as the great galaxies precisely because it is small. When St Augustine declares that the world itself is the greatest miracle, we should conclude that it is an honour to wash our own faces, and that it would not be extravagant to bow down to a leaf. The size of the universe should persuade us how incredibly petty are our own resentments and quarrels, and how stupid our consent to the humdrum.

If our planet and our being are unique in the firmament, that is precisely why they belong. We do not bounce along by chance like a random tennis ball, because the notion of chance implies the notion of uniformity. There is no uniformity in the nature of things. Chance is a deviation from an *expected* course. Newton found a uniformity in the motions of all bodies, but it is at least as important to observe that no two bodies are the same or behave the same: gravity itself differentiates.

A viable philosophy for our day must not have Newtonian space and time as a premise, but must realise the primacy of subjective space and time. We place ourselves in the world, but the placing of the world in us is primary. The spirit is the place of the world. When Confucius maintains that man is the measure of reality, he is not proclaiming any cheap relativism, but realising how profoundly anthropomorphic our knowledge must be. If we confine ourselves to measuring man, and measuring the world in terms of Newtonian space and time, we shall lose ourselves. And this quantification of all things has gone very far. By rocketry we have become obsessed by man in space, forgetting that spirit is the place of the world.

I find resurrection much more plausible than immortality. If the spirit is the body viewed from within, then body and spirit are absolutely united. (Cf. Carl Jung, *Modern Man in Search of a Soul*, pp. 253–4.) To say that body and spirit are absolutely united is not to say that the spirit must die with the body. The body that dies is the opaque body and not the transparent body. The latter grows out of the former like a sprout from a rotted seed. To say that death is the separation of soul and body, and that the former is immortal, is to play the materialist game, for the body here is the opaque body and you cannot have that kind of space without that kind of time. We are thinking on that level, and are tempted to put the immortal soul in

Newtonian time, having put the body into Newtonian space.

To say that every psychic function goes with a bodily modification does not worry me. It seems to me the course of desperation to say that there can be no bodily modification for the higher spiritual functions. We are here still in the realm of secondary thinking. It is unawareness of this that leads to silly questions about the resurrected body: Will we be the same height? Have the same wart on the nose? Have the same coloured hair? These are all questions which imply the observation from without, whereas we should be looking from the inside. The observational stance, which is the stance of Descartes's ego, which mathematicises what we observe, is a stance outside the world because it is outside the body. We see with the angelic eye of the *res cogitans*. The eye which sees the world from within sees it *sub specie aeternitatis*. For this heavenly eye "there is no place and duration, only way and eternity" (Buber, *The Legend of the Baal Shem*, p. 79).

There are some who hold that the "massifying" and manipulation and measuring of men are due to the population explosion. But that is not so. The increase of population is mostly due to the advances in objective science, e.g. advances in medicine and agronomy. This has resulted in the increase of subjects by the million. Then, fatally, we try to deal with this state of affairs by the objective measuring sciences. A social science which reduces these millions to objects seems to me almost macabre. The kind of thinking which produces anaesthetics produces poison gas, and that which produces ploughshares produces swords. We should see in this not a fruitful oscillation but a deadlock. Nature's way of limiting a species should have something to do with the nature of man, namely, to be a subject. Otherwise legions may enter us and we shall plunge by droves into the sea.

Healing men may be a way of killing them, and the source of this ambiguity is the primacy which we give to the subject-object relationship which is coupled with our power-thinking. The efforts of Western medicine to gain control over the human body by Cartesian science remind one of the sorcerer's apprentice. Complications and recondite causalities proliferate until the patient is transformed from a man into a medicated zombie. Chuang-tzu said (T. Merton's translation, pp. 136–7):

> When he tries to extend his power over objects
> Those objects gain control over him.
> He who is controlled by objects
> Loses possession of his inner self.

To the extent that the object of medical science is only *res extensa*, extended matter, it can become an expensive form of homicide. The interpretation of a condition is linear and not total: this leads to this, leads to this, leads to this, and the end is blind. The datum is not taken in the totality of the man, all of whom is present in it. A kidney is never just a kidney – which is a causal, generalising abstraction – but the kidney of John Smith. If the kidney is the Atman's kidney, then *tat tvam asi*, it is also John Smith's liver and lights and a good deal more, and we require more than dissection and analysis to understand the situation. The pathologist needs a macroscope:

> Great knowledge sees all in one.
> Small knowledge breaks down into the many.
> (CHUANG-TZU, P. 40)

Man sustains the cosmos. He is cosmocrator. This sounds ridiculous, as ridiculous as saying that there was a man who is God, who is the creative Logos; and insofar as he draws man into himself man shares in this creative action. When Sartre says, "God did not create Adam, Adam created himself," he is, by Christian standards, too modest. Adam created the universe, but only as co-creator with the Second Adam. When he defects from this vocation, he is in hell, which is the primal chaos. This explains the extraordinary words of the old canon in Denis Saurat's *Death and the Dreamer*, some of which I quote:

> People think that there is a period before Christ, and a period after Christ. That is all nonsense. Everything was created in that instant nine months before the birth of Christ. Of course, after that things had to be put in order; first of all the Very Holy Virgin, so that mankind could be organised around the Word. The Very Holy Virgin is, if you wish to speak historically – always a false way of thinking, mind you – the first created human being ... Creation is spreading ever spreading into the past as into the future.

If we can glimpse that Being is Truth, and that Truth is a Person, the old canon will not seem so crazy. He offsets the quantifiers who make man insignificant, and who would, by their engines, reduce him again to the primal dust, as a stumbling block too great to be endured. *Maya* is not illusion but the measured world, where the measurer stands over against the measured, and does not realise that the source of measurement is his own subjectivity, and that however much as observer he puts himself outside of the picture, his objective knowledge is incurably anthropomorphic, and that that finally means that it is divine.

Creating means to be created, says Martin Buber in *The Legend of the Baal Shem*, so that "if man desires that a new creation comes out of him, then he must come with all his potentiality to the state of nothing, and then God brings forth in him a new creation".

This naughting, to use a word of Julian of Norwich, is not easily borne. We have to go into the dark night to be created again. Our importance comes not only from our grandeur, but also from our misery, and its source is incarnation.

The twentieth-century attitude to the body is a sign of rapidly changing times. From the seventeenth century to our own times a large part of the world has marched under the banner of Puritanism, a word I am using rather widely to cover a contempt of the body, the rejection of a visible Church which goes with it, and a stress on the individual and his immortal soul – and business. That is why Tawney could write *Religion and the Rise of Capitalism*, and Feuerbach *The Essence of Christianity*, which gave so great an impulse to Marx.

It is an interesting piece of historical irony that those who invested so largely in the invisible became foremost in producing and consuming visible goods. A critique of Puritan society in, for instance, South Africa and the U.S.A., must understand the dialectic of Puritanism. Money is the disembodiment of real goods. It becomes the soul of matter, and we wish it to be immortal. This is not the first appearance of this dialectic. St Augustine saw it very clearly in reckoning with the Manichaeans. He sees that sensuality on the one hand, and the contempt of the body on the other, go hand in hand and that what unites them is too much concern with the body, whether negatively or positively. By virtue of this concern, a Puritan culture will breed pornography, and a sensual culture will produce desert hermits.

Disembodied spirit and materialism go together, like Descartes's mind and body, for we have to do here with the consequences of a dualism. The one tends to be reduced to the other, and that is why materialism and idealism in philosophy were born at one birth. Both destroy the significance of the person, which both Marx and Hegel do. It comes to much the same whether we are steamrollered by spirit or matter. Perhaps the former is worse. At any rate St Augustine reminds us that the Devil has no body, and lashes out against those "who carnally seek the spirit and carnally avoid the flesh".

It is understandable that those who have suffered in a culture of disembodied minds should opt for Marx, but Marx is not the answer, for the simple reason that he inherited too much from what he attacked, for instance the centralising of economic control, machine facture, and the implicit atheism of the capitalistic factory system. Perhaps those who have seen further have arrived at the boundary where the Waste Land ends, and where it is possible for persons to live out what they are. Our history since the seventeenth century has now matured and it is plain what issues are at stake. In our generation we are experiencing the terror of being man by the catastrophes which overshadow us; but the very imminence of death may awaken us to our glory. It is no mean being who can hold his death in his hand.

4 : The Desirability of Desire

In philosophic literature you will find a great many different opinions about desire and emotion. Had you gone to a Stoic for counsel, he would possibly have told you to learn *apatheia*, which is a radical extirpation of the desires, in order to achieve invulnerability. St Augustine reacted very strongly to this. Who would not say, he says in *The City of God*, that such a hardness is not worse than sin? Coming from a great Christian theologian this is pretty strong. The emphasis on the sympathetic emotions, which is laid by St Paul, where he tells us to rejoice with those that do rejoice, and weep with those that weep, would be refused by a Stoic on the grounds that it was unworthy. When Jesus heard that Lazarus was dead, he wept most unstoically. Discernment about the ego and its loves is at the very centre of ethics. The Pauline advice is given to those who can step out of their own bounds, and identify with other people. Go where you will in the world and you will find the problems of love and of the ego interwoven.

If we look to the East we shall find that the essence of the Buddha's therapy for the cure of suffering is getting rid of grasping desire. It is griping desire which binds us to the wheel of Samsara. The Stoic therapy is that we shall follow reason. I find this quite unsophisticated. The Buddhist would rather say that we should get beyond reason to the centre of our being where the lotus flowers. We find in the *Tao-te-Ching* the remark that we are wiser than we know and that it is usually better to rely on our hunches than to embark on a reasoning process, which is too often guided by our self-centredness and unadmitted prejudices. We are speaking here of the reason of rationalism, and not of the reason of Aristotle or St Thomas, whose "reason" embraces the body and the psyche. Hence the Taoist emphasis on *wu-wei*, sitting still and doing nothing, so that subliminal forces may take over.

The students of Buddhism very soon come up against the question whether all desire is grasping desire, which encloses us in our own egos. It is true that Buddhism goes very far in its analysis of egohood and its desires, and lays great emphasis on detachment. When it teaches the absolute perishability of the self, it points out that our desire for immortality is simply a selfish grasping of our ego, which loves itself too much to be willing to let go. We must accept death in relaxed hands.

We have to remember, however, how saturated with desire we are. The *conatus suum esse conservare* is an obbligato to the existence of any being. The failing of desire in a pathologically depressed person is very near intolerable. There seems to be no motive for anything. One can hardly collect the strength to put one's shoes on. The Hassid, Leib, who visited a great Zaddik, which we may call a Jewish guru, declared,

> I came to the Maggid not to listen to discourses, nor to

learn from his wisdom; I came to watch him tie his shoelaces.

Desire fails, and the grasshopper becomes a burden. Desire is constitutive of the "now" and if it fails the "now" is intolerable. When saints tell us to live in the "now", they cannot mean this condition. There is a false and a true living in the present and with each goes a certain kind of ego. The Buddhist wishes to get rid of grasping desire which negates the present for the future, and the incapsulated ego that goes with it. But there are desires which are not grasping, and selves which are not self-idolatrous. In any event we are committed to desiring. *Nemo est qui non amet*, says St Augustine, but we must take heed of the quality of our loves.

That is why there are for St Augustine two kinds of *amor sui*, a saving kind which is the norm supposed in the injunction to love our neighbour as we love ourselves; and the selfish kind, the *amor concupiscentiae*, orientated entirely to the satisfaction of our own egos. This goes along with his discrimination of goods which are unitive and divisive, of goods which are increased by sharing and of those which are lessened. For instance, if I impart my knowledge to someone, my knowledge is not halved, but increased, while if I give my tobacco, I have so much the less tobacco. The need for law arises from the clash of divisive desires.

In the contemporary fugue into the Oriental, we may be tempted to forget how great was the medieval Christian contribution to the analysis of the desires. Medieval men recognised three great lusts: the *cupido sentiendi*, the *cupido sciendi*, and the *cupido dominandi*: the lusts of feeling, of knowing, and of empire. They are called lusts because they run to excess, and rule us because they create in us idolatrous loves. It is this idolatry which pulls them out of context. It is right to feel, to know and to govern. It is wrong to make them ends in themselves, and to evert the hierarchy of temperance.

The Renaissance unchained these lusts, which are all forms of the *cupido habendi*, the lust of possession, which had a fresh chance to bloom in the Renaissance. When the West Indies were opened, when the geographical and stellar bounds were broken, men unleashed the infinite in themselves and dreamt of unending riches and power and rule. One could not find a better recipe for war. There have always been wars sparked off by these egoisms, but the most remarkable dimension of their growth occurred in the *cupido sciendi*, the lust of science, which could provide new weapons of war, and new sources of delectation.

Contemporaries were well aware of what was happening. Among others, Marlowe anatomised these lusts in his plays: avarice in *The Jew of Malta*, empire in *Tamburlaine*, and, above all, science in *Faustus*, and indeed our own age is a Faustian age, where we have so much knowledge without wisdom, so many goods without temperance, and so great an empire over nature. We shall exploit men as long as we go on exploiting nature. Indeed, we shall exploit ourselves, for by our lusts we reduce ourselves to slavery.

When Bacon spoke of the enlarging of the bounds of human empire, to the effecting of all things possible, he did not appreciate the possibility of the reduction of men to things. The shades of Christianity still hid this from him, and there is something monkish or priestlike about the researchers in Salomon's House. He sees nothing ominous in the quantification of the objects of desire which this institution is to accomplish.

Those who think that Buddhism contains the answer to all their problems, fail to see the strength of their own tradition. While Buddhist pundits were hairsplitting grasping desire into many dozens of variety, Western thinkers were analysing the political consequences of grasping desire. The foremost was St Augustine, who, finding the roots of grasping desire in pride, built the *Civitas Terrena*, the Devil's Kingdom, out of the bricks of our egoism. This is the tradition of the Old Testament, which finds the evidence of God in history, and of Plato when he says that we can apply moral predicates to societies as well as to individuals. We can call both men and societies just or unjust, so that there is no gap between ethics and politics.

This gap is a post-medieval invention. The virtue of Machiavelli's Prince is completely removed from private virtue. The *cupido dominandi* is virtue in a prince. When Mandeville argues that private vices are public benefits, he could hardly be further from both the Greek and the Christian traditions. I say "hardly" because there is still one point of contact: a concern with the connection between private and political action, even if it is now negatively treated. Desire still has a political dimension, and the statesman and lawgiver have a responsibility in respect of it.

It would be hard to deny that government, today also, has a vested interest in private vice and in exploitation, insofar as there is an overlap between governmental power and money power. Things are in the saddle, so that there is a proliferation of undesirable desires. Both political and psychological conflict arise from these desires. Shocking as we may find the Inquisition or modern brainwashing, they have one virtue: they recognise the relevance of the inner to the outer life. It is the homage of vice to virtue. Buddhism is not a persecuting religion, but we may perhaps keep our minds open as to whether that is altogether in its favour. I say this because our *yang* period is sure to usher in a *yin* period, when we may be disposed to undervalue our empirical science and its politics.

Law is concerned with the situations which arise from the desires of men, from the clash, very often, between what they want and what they need; and the desires of men arise from their temporal condition. Man is never all that he is. In the language of the existentialists, his being is a to-be. Man endeavours to discover and to be what he is, and this takes time. He desires because he is *not yet* what he wants to be, and what he wants to be is what lies covered in the present: himself. Our sense of the future rests upon the quality of our desire. The *amor concupiscentiae* creates a different future and a different legislative programme from the *amor Dei*, because they place our human being in different times. Legislation for eternity and legislation for time correspond to two different qualities of desire; and my contention is that legislation for eternity will be found to be legislation for the times, and that this is just the opposite of legislation for time, which reflects the hopelessness of a desire which has no dialectic of ascent.

Society progressively reveals to us what we are and therefore what we want. And if we do not learn to want ourselves but evacuate the centre, the rotation of the sun and the passage of time itself are infected with this boredom. Insofar as legislation has to do with the situations which arise from desires of men, it also has to do with situations which create proper or improper desires; and from the point of view of the ontologist, there is a fundamental angle on lawmaking, which regards it as an activity by which human time is constructed. For it can construct hopeful and hopeless situations, and a hopeless situation is essentially one in which time has lost its meaning, and in which desire has failed.

The philosophy of law, then, would do well to concern itself with the ontology of time, on the grounds that legislation has to do with the construction of human time, i.e. with the construction of historical and of subjective time. Thus legislation might be called bad when it constructed the time of frustration, or anxiety, or boredom, concepts which the reader of St Augustine or Kierkegaard should have no difficulty in understanding. There is such a thing as a sophistic time of nihilism in which human acts are performed which are stripped of all meaning. St

Augustine's conception of the *Civitas Terrena* depends upon the conception of such a time, the time of idolatry in which creatures are stripped of significance by being blown up into false infinities or false eternities. If Maritain, following St Thomas, is right in saying that the practical judgement must be *per conformitatem ad appetitum rectum*, i.e. *de corde pura*, then we had better be serious about the nature of the *appetitum rectum*, or lawful desire.

In fact, we may wonder whether society does not exist for creating desires rather than for satisfying them. There is a ladder of loves, and at last we desire something, which can never be temporally satisfied, an eternal reality. True love, for Plato, leads to an aristocracy of intelligence, false loves to the tyrannical state which is the lowest kind of rat race, in which the love of friendship disappears. The Greek reverence for Harmodius and Aristogeiton rests on the belief that the love of friendship overthrows tyrannies. In the *Symposium* Plato sets out a scale of loves, each lower love being taken up into a higher love until the form of Beauty is seen with the inward eye, as something implicit in all loves.

We can talk, then, of a dialectic of desire in which desire finds its true nature and its proper object. This is totally different from the mere quantification of desire, which is what we have so largely aimed at in our technological society. As Plato and St Augustine saw, this quantification knows no limit. It sets up false infinities, and leads to the idolisation of the ego and of money. This is tied up with the process of mass production, which requires mass-consumption, which in turn requires the advertiser who whips up desires for material possessions.

A curious irony comes into operation here. We want to become the masters and possessors of nature, to take it in hand and dominate it with no limit, because we have desacralised it.

> Instead of being given, as in Plato's pedagogic ideal, what they *ought* to have, the masses are being scientifically studied as to what they *want* to have, and this is being poured in an unending stream, chemically into expectant mouths and electronically into expectant eyes. Thus, while the philosophers of 'mid-culture' proclaim man's final liberation from the childlike dependence on faith, the managers of mass-culture create forms of infantile dependence on an unheard-of scale, a primitive form of passivity.
>
> (KARL STERN, *THE FLIGHT FROM WOMAN*, PP. 301–2)

From being the masters and possessors of nature, they have become enslaved to the senses and to those who manipulate them. This manipulated mass, to persuade itself that it is still dominant, invents democracy which is supported rather by a readiness to swallow than by a capacity to create. Maximisation of knowledge and of desire is not wisdom. Equality of men = predictability of consumers. Thus this equality is not a spiritual insight but an exigency of technology, not a freedom but a condition of servitude. As Karl Stern (p. 293) remarks on Goethe's *Faust*, "Faust knew a thousand times *more* than Margaret but she knew a thousand times *better* than he." Multiplicity of desires creates servitude and not strength. Little desires smother qualitatively great desires, and make moral and other genius impossible.

When Plato, in the *Republic*, discusses the process of democratising desires, we should do well to take some heed. The spiritual aristocrat is a flame and not a box of matches – nor a thousand matches in a registry office. You can mass-produce sex but not love, and this lies at the bottom of the divorce problem, which is a problem of quantification, which has no dialectic upwards, though it has a kind of dialectic of decay. The H-bomb is the ejaculation of a sick society.

> *Wirr wissen nicht was wir brauchen, wir brauchen nicht was wir wissen.*
> (GOETHE)

St Augustine, even more than Plato, knows that man desires an ultimate fusion of love and intelligence. "Thou hast made us for Thyself, and our hearts are restless till they find rest in Thee," says St Augustine in a famous passage in the *Confessions*, a passage which will remain alive when all the linguistic analysers of God-talk are forgotten.

But what I find so very important in St Augustine is his teaching that at the heart of every desire, no matter how sinful, there is a seed of the divine radiance which can be set free. I think that that is why he is so vehement against the Stoics. What is called for is not an extirpation of desire, even sinful desire, but the removal of the husks which hide the light. Better a powerful sinner than a *frigidus*, and that may be some excuse for Luther's famous *pecca fortiter et crede firmius*. St Augustine's own *Confessions* reveal a dialectic of desire. He had loved fame and women, and as the husks were peeled off these desires they were not destroyed but burnt with a clear flame, an oblation of fire.

He was not so foolish as to try to substitute reasons for passion, and I think he would have regarded it as absolutely misguided to prefer a mere concept of God to a vital carnality. He never did things by halves, and he was a passionate lover all his life. He did not entertain pallid doubts as to whether God was alive or dead. He went straight to experience. "O love, ever burning and never extinguished, charity, my God, set me on fire." (*Confessions*, X. 29) He would have understood this sentence from "The Splendid Tale of Prince Diamond" in *The Arabian Nights*: "[Allah] who has set woman before the eyes of man and has planted desire in his heart, a jewel within a stone."

> Nor should a person become depressed by his sins, for this is Satan's device for separating us even further from God. The holy sparks of God are hidden everywhere, even in sinful situations; how else could there be any pleasure in sin? Instead of despairing a sinner must 'lift the holy sparks' out of their uncongenial surroundings and into a place where their joy-giving qualities can be more fully released.
>
> (H. WEINER, *THE KABBALA TODAY*, P. 127)

I suppose that in counselling one is trying to chip the jewel out of the matrix. Since every nature is a Buddha nature, Buddhist meditation too is concerned with sweeping off the rubble. I think that the positions which I have set before you have some practical value. One is trying to crack the hard nut and set something free. One has to penetrate and expand the desires to unfold the lotus bud. Most moral and psychological trouble arises from egocentricity. There is a lot of it often in the desire to be a certain kind of self. We can't make a blueprint for ourselves and try to live it out. We should probably fall into some kind of rationalist trap. We cannot do other people's meditation for them, but perhaps we can persuade them that they are living and growing, and that we cannot programme an orange tree to bear apples. We have to find out what we are, and expand what is given.

The Augustinian attitude to desire has many echoes. Thus A.J. Heschel in *The Passion for Truth* writes of the Baal Shem Tov:

> Before the Baal Shem's time, pious Jews felt that to be close to God, the body must be chastised, one must fast and scourge oneself. Bodily enjoyment was considered despicable, sexual pleasures filled them with revulsion. But the Baal Shem and his followers held that all delights come from Eden.

A longing for things material is an instrument by which one may approach the love of God, and even through coarse desires one may come to love the creator. Lust, desire, evil inclination, all should be elevated, not uprooted.

Contrast the Dhyana Sutra, which is a Buddhist classic:

> The continual sufferings of birth and death are due to thy sensual desires and lusts. When these thy children are grown they become thine enemies, and all thy laborious work has been in vain, and after the last breath thou art buried in the grave.
>
> How foul is thy dead body; how putrid is a dead corpse: Its nine cavities yield stinking fluids, but thou, O fool, clingest to it as does a maggot to excrement.

I do not know, and should be glad to be told, how far counselling is supposed to go. A Christian spiritual director or a Buddhist guru would set us the goal of enlightenment, and I presume that a wise counsellor would not wish merely to make us efficient in the rat race, or to paint us the same colour as our surroundings.

I have often tried to get it across that the world is ours because it isn't, or, if you like, that the only attachment is detachment. But that is a long story which I am not going to tell now.

Perhaps I should end with this apparent paradox, but I should like to unravel it just a little. The great spiritual counsellors have always advised detachment. One thinks of Christ's advice to the young man to sell all his goods. Does this mean that a man should take no interest in his family, his dog, his house, his furniture? That it should be so I should find hard to credit. But I should like to point out that at the level of ordinary consciousness the attachment-detachment poles are in full operation.

I say: that is a chair there. We call the chair an object. It is *there*. But for it to be there, there must be a *here*, to which the chair is relative. The chair has been *ob-jected* by us. I have distanced it. It is *not me*. I can form a concept of it, penetrate its essence, use and make it. It is close to me because I have distanced myself from it. I think it is in this sense that the Buddhist declares that the world is mind.

If you keep your distance from it, forget the subject, concentrate only on the object, you get modern objective science. Then we may forget that every object requires a subject, a *here* which distances the object, but at the same time draws it into itself. Any chair, the whole world, is mine because I can say it is a not-me, and so attach it to me. I am closer to the chair than any animal can be. That is why Aquinas says that the mind can become all things, and why the Buddhist says that we must keep the mind a clear mirror. We are all attached and that attachment we can never break.

But what happens then to the counsel of detachment, which is a spiritual counsel and not an epistemological statement? I wish to suggest that the saint's detachment is really a higher form of attachment, and that his world is brighter than our ordinary world because he can stand further back from it and get it in clearer focus. When St Francis talks about "brother sun", the fraternal attachment is a superior detachment because the sun properly focused is seen to be a creature of God, primarily God's because all creatures, the ten thousand things, are God's, given to us, and therefore ours because fundamentally they are not ours, so that we can at any moment give them back with open hands.

Detachment, then, is not cutting loose from things, or reducing them to a kind of miasma, but seeing them in their native brilliance, closer to them than ever before, because they are not our property but our brothers and sisters. The tyrant or tycoon hogs the world because he hogs his own ego, the ego of grasping desire. That is the kind of desire which leads to false attachment, attachment also to the grasping ego. Detachment requires that we sit loose also to ourselves, losing ourselves, losing the world, only to experience that they are given new. This is not the extirpation of desire, but its transformation into a love which has no fear that it may lose its object. When the Buddhist says: let your *samsara* be your *nirvana*, or when Plato speaks of the intuition of beauty, this is what they appear to me to mean.

There are various kinds of detachment. There is the detachment of the scientists, which has to be practised to keep the phenomena investigated pure. I should call this a kind of absent presence, which constitutes the phenomenon an object, and sets up Buber's I-it relationship. This impersonal attitude to the object requires that it be present to us, but not that it be a presence *for* us, the latter constituting Buber's I-Thou relationship.

Now how can there be, at the same time, both presence *and* detachment? A psychologist has to be objective about his patient, but on the other hand if he is not a presence to him, counselling would be in vain. Are detachment, and objectivity in the above sense, incompatible? Has the detached man to be impersonal?

Let us take the instance of a *guru* and his *chela*. Now a guru is not one who gives his novice teaching only. He is not, like most university professors, giving knowledge only. He is giving himself. Initiation is a gift of the guru to the novice, and sets up a very close personal relationship. Christ also taught detachment, but he loved John. Jesus and John were presences to each other, we might say: attached to each other. But John could not receive the Holy Spirit, which is the love of God, until Jesus had departed. It seems as though utter detachment and utter love go together. Undue attachment is idolatry. To idolise one's wife and children is a failure in love. Real love is to see them for what they are and for what they can be. There is nothing less blind than love, and nothing is of harder steel than charity. It was St Teresa of Avila who said that it is not wonderful that God should have so few friends when you consider how he treats them.

And yet religion is the practice of the presence of God, whose presence is simply the present, and the practice of accepting the present.

> Giving oneself over to the here and now without reservation or hesitation results in a perfect expression of spontaneity.
> (CALM AND CLEAR, P. 98)

Immersion in the present would then, and beyond all ordinary expectation, be the supreme detachment.
> Not to be attached to something is to be aware of its absolute value.
> (SHUNOYA SUZUKI, *Zen Mind, Beginner's Mind*, P. 62)

This is the ripeness of emotional experience, and the fulfilment of all desire. The desire which is a fugue into the past or the future is deeply destructive.

It is by desire that we create reality. God so loved the world ... and this love is his act of Creation in which we share. The man who quantifies desire has one world; the man who ascends the ladder of love, the *scala amoris,* another. According to Plato love and intelligence become one in the vision of the Good and the Beautiful. The highest reality within our experience is ourselves and other people. How we relate to them is constitutive of our reality, and this relatedness is primarily through our desire and aversion, the latter being a desire to get away from something. Hate uncreates the world and opens the primal abyss where time as the procession of creatures vanishes, and the desire for ourselves, which is the desire for life, disappears. We are left with desire after desire which ceaseth only in death, so that our lives are lived in the time of fear.

And so, to conclude, counselling has, at any rate largely, to concern itself with the subjective time-structure of the patient, and his conversion from the desires which set up a false time-system; and from an ego which, in clutching itself, makes both presence and detachment impossible.

4 : THE DESIRABILITY OF DESIRE

The following quotations sum up what I wish to say:
To the man in ecstasy the habitual is eternally new. A Zaddik stood at the window in the early morning light and trembling cried: 'A few hours ago it was night and now it is day – God brings up the day.' And he was full of fear and trembling. He also said: 'Every creature should be ashamed before the Creator: were he perfect, as he was destined to be, then he would be astonished and awakened and inflamed because of the renewal of the creature at each time and in each moment.'
(M. BUBER, THE LEGEND OF THE BAAL SHEM, P. 18)

In ecstasy all that is past and that is future draws near to the present. Time shrinks, and the line between the eternities disappears; only the moment lives, and the moment is eternity. In its undivided light appears all that was and all that will be, simple and composed.
(BUBER, P. 20)

5 : The Yin and the Yang in Christian Culture*

Many of us would experience a certain embarrassment on being asked whether we were Christians, and this would arise not only from a sense of privacy invaded, or from an erosion of belief, but from certain doubts about many current so-called Christian attitudes, which we would certainly not wish to seem to confess. In fact, we are all under the influence of the Christian ethic and spirituality, and inevitably go on being Christian as Chinese go on being Confucian, no matter what sea changes have occurred. The Marxist, for instance, continues to be dynamised by much of what he explicitly rejects. You can take stock of where you are, but you cannot step out of it, and I wish here to consider some of the factors which cause the embarrassment, principally the factors which have led to an exaggerated masculinisation of our culture.

Now, Christianity is not a pure Platonic essence laid up in heaven, though we hear enough of the essence of Christianity, of pure Gospel Christianity, of uncontaminated primitive Christianity, or what have you, to suspect that many think that it is. Loyalty to the Church for many

---

* In Chinese philosophy, *yin* and *yang*, feminine and masculine, receptive and domineering, are a fundamental tension in reality.

is a loyalty based on the belief that the Church has its boarding hooks fixed in this essence, but this is to miss the point of an incarnated church.

Christ himself was a Jew, with a Jewish background and habits, and, while he may be the everlasting man, it is not because he is, as it were, the Form of Man, but because every man must have a race, colour, and background. What is perennial is a lack of perennial fixity. To be a Christian cannot possibly mean to conform to a type or to coincide with the paradigm case. And if you are asked by anybody with such an idea in the back of his mind, whether you are a Christian, it is intensely embarrassing. You may say no, not because you are a Judas but because you are trying not to be.

In fact I find the word Christianity, to the extent that it suggests fixities of this kind, rather odd, and the phrase, Christian religion, odder still, at any rate insofar as religion carries with it a suggestion of decorum, of prescribed ways, and a manner of conservatism. If religion is connected with the notion of *ligare*, it may be a bit of a bind.

I suppose that one of the reasons why the Christian religion has an official approval in our society is that it is regarded as the custodian of the decencies, which often means the set ways. At any rate, most innovations, like telescopes, railway trains, the Galilean hypothesis, labour unions and votes for women have encountered some *soi-disant* Christian opposition. I won't mention revolutions: they are so upsetting to the Stock Exchange and to the Insurance Companies, those pillars of the Christian West.

But what one discerns in Christ is an uprush of new life which broke up the old forms and the old decencies. He undermined the old association between religion and money, symbolised by money changers in the temple, which was a characteristic of his own society as it is of ours. I noticed a great deal of churchgoing in the United States, and one wonders whether it is because the Americans are Christians or because they are affluent. At any rate, they don't like Marx's or Veblen's answer to the question.

But my point is that Jesus was no centre of decorum. I am not suggesting for a moment that he was ill-mannered. No doubt he behaved well at table, and was clued up on what is done at weddings. His mother would have seen to that. But you could hardly invoke him in support of a Sunday Observance Act, and the dreary proprieties that go with it. He showed respect but never respectability. How strange that he should have become the centre of a cult to which it is respectable to belong! How strange that his name should be protected by blasphemy laws, when he himself was accused of blasphemy, and when the criterion for the application of the law seems to be the degree to which the verbal proprieties of the community are outraged. This man ate with publicans and sinners. He was, from a certain point of view, improper, and his crime was to attack the ecclesiastical authorities who were the guardians of what was prudent and well established, in fact, for criticising the goodness of his society.

We are so accustomed to hearing that it was our sins

which crucified Christ, and that he died both for and by our sins, that we do not pause to reflect on what those sins were. It was the priests and the Pharisees who were the rabble-rousers. It was the "good" men, in the Nietzschean sense of the term, who engineered the crucifixion. It was not the thieves and publicans and prostitutes, except insofar as they are the inevitable parts of a respectable society. The rulers also disapproved of thieves. They crucified Christ between two of them, and if he died for them, it was because he was dying for that sort of oligarchic goodness which forces some men to steal.

Let us be clear on this point. It was "good" men who crucified Christ. Is it so very wrong to object to a man calling himself God? It seems to be of the essence of religion to object to this, and it is the gravamen of our charge against the Communists. Is it unreasonable or imprudent to decide that one man should die for the people? We act on that principle when we imprison or hang a murderer, when a Pope compromises with the Nazis on the persecution of the Jews for the safety of the whole church, or when Rome silences a controversial writer so that the so-called little ones shall not be scandalised!

So perhaps it is our goodness which we must confess, and crucify from day to day, and perhaps the real fruit of original sin is the compulsion under which we are to be good and to establish a workable order of society with all its relative and prudential goodnesses. And perhaps that is the problem with which St Augustine was struggling in the *De Civitate Dei*. Seneca remarked of wives that we couldn't live with them and we couldn't live without them. Is that true of Christ? I feel rather sorry for the priests and Pharisees. It would be hypocritical to regard them as monsters of iniquity. They were very like the Pope and the Curia, and if I were more like Christ I should have more sympathy with them. When you get a Christ-like Pope, like John XXIII, he upsets the political order of the church quite considerably.

I have used the phrase "like Christ" and this brings me to the difficult question of the imitation of Christ. Here again, as always, we land in paradox. Of course we should be like Christ, and of course we can't and shouldn't be. Where do I start imitating, and where do I stop? Have I to become a carpenter, and learn Aramaic, and aspire to working miracles? Nonsense! Well, where do I start imitating, and where do I stop? I, for one, find Christ inimitable. I would call your attention to the fact that this opens a very general question. Every man is inimitable by virtue of being a person. We can't step into his mother's womb, nor receive the impressions nor repeat the circumstances which have made him what he is. And yet we cannot live without taking the impress of other people. A man is fortunate if he has a good father and mother to imitate. And yet the very excellence of the exemplar may be a liability. It gives rise to the mother-in-law question.

Many a son has been crippled by idealising his father, and many a son has been wrecked because his father has presumed to set his course for him. One cannot live a life which is a pastiche. The difficulty crops up all over the place. If we do not like the art of Luini it is because he follows Leonardo too closely. One may, and should, admire Kierkegaard and Nietzsche in philosophy, but neither wanted followers, but only hearers. I can conceive of nothing more alien to the spirit of St Thomas than the slavish respect which some have accorded to Scholastic philosophy. He was a great innovator in philosophy and theology, and yet we use him to curb innovation, as though he had said the last word. Imitate St Francis and become a sentimentalist about animals. It is wrong imitation which has wrecked so much church art, and church morals which come straight out of the repository.

I am thinking, for instance, of plaster-cast purity. Two twiddles and it's a venial sin; three twiddles and it's masturbation. Rhythm and it's right; the pill and it's wrong. Is that Christian morals? Good God! You might as well ask if some holy cards are Christian art. And there is a connection. Real morals produce real art, and the stuff with which we decorate our churches is a direct indication of the degree of our moralism. Imitation art and imitation morals go hand in hand. I mention also the shirking of responsibility which often lies behind the question, what would you do if you were in my place? And what of the question, what would Christ do if he were in my place? Well, I don't know. I might as well ask how he would write this piece! Something more surprising than I could ever contrive. I am sure he often surprised himself. That is the reward of a creator, and he was the supreme creator, in morals as well.

So we treat him as we have treated, for instance, St Thomas, and use him as a bulwark against all innovation. After all, we say, the church is the repository of revelation. Maybe. There is a sense in which I feel sure that this is true. But a coffin is also a repository, and Christ broke the bonds of death. How much that is iniquitous has been covered by the phrase "repository of revelation"? For here, too, there is a contradiction. This revelation was the irruption of something new, a refreshing of all history, and of all creation, and immediately we set to work to make it something old, something which is to be used to combat all change, something which is to be eternal in the sense of being rigid.

We take the baby and we put it in a coffin instead of in a cradle. We imitate Lot's wife instead of Jesus, and we turn behaviour into a principle of retrospection instead of prospection. The Marxist then steps into the vacuum which we have created, and insists on the relativity of morals, and the need to orientate society to the future. And he falls into the same trap. Marx and Lenin are the eternal word, and all deviationists must be examined by the Curia. The trouble about the Curia and the Party is that they are too much like each other, and on that level the Party has the advantage.

I seem to be going a long way round to say that if there is not a timeless Christianity, neither can you reduce the life with Christ to a code of rules. You cannot reduce the

Sermon on the Mount to a set of commands, valid and intelligible for all peoples at all times. Again you cannot send a *fiat* of monogamy abroad in total disregard of local customs and traditions, nor expect modesty in dress to mean the same thing to an Eskimo as to a Congo pygmy. I am still in the dark as regards St Paul's recipe for becoming all things to all men. One would like to be able to compare his epistle to the pygmies with his epistle to the Eskimos. St Paul going pygmy is too much for the imagination.

We seem to have to accept that Christianity is something which is modified by history but still has in it something that can appeal against that modification; a something which you cannot describe as an eternal essence or a trans-historical code of rules, a self-rectifying tendency which is perhaps the Holy Spirit? I am protesting only against the many human forms of ossifying the spirit.

The critique of the modification sets in when a stereotype becomes settled, and the stereotype of the modern world has been the domination complex or the individualistic assumption. They are related. I have a protest to make against the *yang*, or dominative phase of our Christianity.

A change in Christianity takes place at the beginning of the modern world, a change on so many fronts that I can advert here only to a small fraction of the spectrum. It modified itself consonantly with the total modification of Western culture. The *Zeitgeist* is all-embracing, and not to be despised. This constitutes no criticism of early modern

Christianity. It tried to be relevant, as it has always tried to be relevant. The feudal form of Christianity wears the colours of history as plainly as Calvinism, and while it has its excellences it cannot be extolled as though, through it, the Essence had come fully down to earth.

From the time of the Incarnation place and time have had their say, and we have to make allowance for them even in the Gospels, which we must relate, for instance, to current literary forms, according to our knowledge of the latter, which we cannot claim to be complete. They are easy to understand only while we are naive and assertive enough not to relativise our own interpretation. The capacity to relativise our own interpretation is a form of humility and a mark of the cultured mind. It is the literalists who are the best clue to the *Zeitgeist* because they have not been conscious of the mesh through which they have sieved the word. They have sacrificed objectivity to objectivism.

The thread which I wish to pick up is the trail of some of the effects of late medieval nominalism on Christian culture. The effect of nominalism was to fragment nature and society into such a manifold that reason cannot hold these together, so that the mind itself becomes fragmented. One comes to despair of wisdom and the metaphysical universe. The invisible connections and universal groupings which thought discerns come to seem unreal and we are left with disparate matter, disparate sensations, and disparate men, of which, being human, we wish to make some sense and about which we desire some certainty.

Enter the spirit of *Yang*. If in nature we can truly apprehend only disparate individuals, then the image of God in it is gone, together with any speculative attempt to weld them into a whole. The only thing that we can do about nature is to do something to it. We can collect and collate our experiences of individuals, not to disclose an eternal pattern, but, like the prisoners in Plato's cave, to predict with the highest probability which way the cat will jump next. That enables you to lay your bets. It enables you to *use* nature for the purpose of satisfying your desires, desires which in the hands of an ultranominalist like Hobbes are themselves disparate, and can be welded only into an artificial unity, and used. Capitalist production was to effect the latter. It stimulated the desires which increase consumption.

We should notice the effect of this on our conception of causality. Only efficient causality remains respectable. You notice that one thing happens, and then, in a linear time series, another thing happens. If the observations of the sequence are invariable, you have a law, regarded as a statement of necessary sequence. Causality becomes a matter of linear sequence, and if you quantify your observations, you have succeeded in mechanising nature completely. What happens follows completely from what happened before, and time *is* the linear succession of the necessarily determined. *Kairos* yields completely to *chronos*. You can construct a chronometer, but a kairometer would be a rather different matter.

In any event, that gives you one kind of certainty, and

the men of the seventeenth century were obsessed with mathematical certainty. In a time of change and ecclesiastical disintegration, men also sought for religious and moral certainty. Some, like Descartes and Spinoza, called in geometry to the aid of moral certainty. But a great many more took refuge in a literally inspired Bible, clear to the meanest understanding, or at any rate capable of codification into exact maxims of behaviour. This was the Protestant *yang* reaction, which reached one of its summits at Geneva. The corresponding Catholic *yang* reaction was the Council of Trent. In either event you had an uprush of moralism and legalism. Neither the mechanistic philosophers nor the divines left room for spontaneity. One listened to Father. In Geneva you experienced all the compulsions of efficient causality. Both in science and morals there is a carnival of law.

The attempt to unify the disparate is pervasive. One of the ways of dealing with the fragmentation of nature was to find a divine lawgiver who arbitrarily decreed the regularity of nature by laws which did not express the natures of the things related but the decisions of Nature's God. Hume did not need that hypothesis but found the source of law in the necessary, and in that sense arbitrary, mechanisms of the human imagination. In politics Machiavelli translated political prudence into the calculation of forces. It is the heyday of the absolute ruler, King Yang alias Leviathan, who gathers the scattered dust of individuals into a lawful society, though his laws are as artificial as those of the social contract. Like the God of Deism, or the literal

5 : THE YIN AND THE YANG IN CHRISTIAN CULTURE

inspirer of the Bible, he originates the code. You have a culture nearly all the elements of which are tarred with the same brush: the dominance of the father image.

The reduction of nature to a linear causal series, in which events are located in Newtonian time, enables us to reduce the knowledge of nature to a quantitative science of movement. It enables us to predict and control movement and in that sense to become the masters and possessors of nature. As Hobbes puts it,

> To build castles, houses, temples; to move, carry, take away mighty weights; to send securely over seas; to contrive engines, etc. ... is to be learnt from reasoning."*

In this view our science is the science of moving things, including ourselves, and in our time it has received the sort of vindication of which it is capable by our landing men on the moon. It has enabled us to follow the Baconian blueprint of manipulating nature to the effecting of all things possible. Salomon's House has taken root all over the world. Science, beyond the dreams of any magician, has articulated the Word of Power.

This masculine urge to dominate could come to its fullest expression by the aid of the machine, orientated to producing things useful for the delectation of the nation and

---

* Hobbes, *Opera Omnia*, ed. Molesworth, 268; quoted in ch. 12 of my *Mirror of Philosophers*, which is very relevant to this theme.

the profit of the machine owner. There are a few things we might notice here. Delectation or pleasure – things are useful if they give pleasure – becomes tied up with machine-facture, which thrives to the extent that it can produce pleasure-giving utilities. If it is profitable to persuade men to increase their desires and to look upon themselves as consumer-machines of pleasure-giving articles, to that extent machine-facture will flourish and profits soar.

Had Hobbes set out to be the domestic philosopher of the new capitalism he could not have made out a more brilliant case for justifying and furthering it. His combination of mechanism and hedonism is complete, even to the drawing of the conclusion that, since pleasures are enjoyed in the linear time of abstract causality, life is a meaningless succession of pleasure after pleasure which ceaseth only in death.

We should notice further that we cannot master nature by industrial processes, unless some men are masters over others. The exploitation of nature becomes the exploitation of some men by other men, who are nevertheless still required to consume the products. The profits of the machine owner are moreover to be reckoned in quantitative mathematical terms: so much of an abstract symbol called money. If we ever get so far as to ask what money is for, our logic compels us to answer: pleasure.

But there is a truth, as certain as Newton's law, that you cannot oppress others without oppressing yourself. Its manifestation here is connected with a curious translation of hedonism into rigorism. Very long ago St Augustine pointed out that hedonism and Manichaean puritanism had a common root: a too great concern with the bodily, so that the one could easily swing over into the other. And much longer ago Plato, in Book VIII of the *Republic*, described how the money-making man, under the pressure of making more money, was compelled to oppress his desires and assume a cloak of moralistic respectability which covered a deep inner division.

The times of Hobbes are the times of the Puritans, and perhaps he disliked them so much because the worst feuds are family feuds. Like Plato's oligarch, the puritan was successful in business and came under the need, which Plato has so well analysed, to oppress himself.* In a pamphlet in the employment bureau for students of my university there was a slogan in fat type: you can't drive others if you do not drive yourself. That is what we are talking about. A deep contradiction reveals itself: money may be for pleasure, and rest on the production of pleasure-giving objects, but to make a lot of money you must take time off from pleasure. Indeed, you must be ascetic. You must drive yourself along the strait and narrow road which leads to acquisition.

It is interesting that there was a revival of both Epicureanism and Stoicism in the sixteenth and seventeenth centuries, but the entrepreneur class, to which socially the clerics also belonged, naturally wished to baptise this self-

---

* See the chapter "Morals and Moralism" in my *Persons*.

oppression as Christian. Hence you get a Stoic and legalist approach to the Bible. God is the Newton of the moral world, and perhaps the clue to Newton's interest in Biblical interpretation lies here. Viewing nature as he did through the eyes of his law, he felt an affinity with the Author of the Book. At any rate the divines and the business class who supported Cromwell wished you to grasp that too much concern with your "lower" nature was sin. You must abide by the law as it is unambiguously proclaimed in Scripture. If not you have guilt, and the technique of preaching shall be to arouse feelings of guilt and a conviction of sin. A Wesley could do that very well. A carnival of *Yang*!

Together with this goes the phenomenon of the closed or constricted ego, or what might be called the individualist assumption. It, too, is rooted in a nominalist world. The individual alone is real, and any relations into which he may enter have the character of impositions. Universals are figments, hence social wholes and social relations have an artificial character. The reality is egoism. Anonymity is at a discount, and what you must do is make a name for yourself. You do that by the exercise of power. As Hobbes remarked, what makes both you and others esteem you is power. One recalls here Plato's analysis of sophistry, and his conclusion that, insofar as sophistry is power-seeking, it is a phenomenon of sheer egoism incapable of entering into dialogue. It subverts the communal good.

This takes the form of individualism not only in business and politics, but also in religion, and constitutes the problem of a corporate and unified Church. The Catholic conception of the Church and of the papal primacy suffers a severe blow, and again the Bible comes to be looked on as a law book which can step into the shoes of the older discipline. The printing machines could produce plenty of Bibles though they could not, at that time at any rate, mass-produce a uniformity of interpreters. Salvation becomes an individual rather than a corporate matter, the saving of your soul a matter of private enterprise. One of the marks of this is the emphasis laid upon the immortality of the individual soul, so that in the eighteenth century Boswell and Johnson were to agree that this was the greatest hope that Christianity had bestowed on mankind. Observe what this contains: the continuation of the soul in a linear or Newtonian time. Eternal life is long life, or, if you like, a good life-expectation.

Since Newtonian time is the time of the entrepreneur, it was a religion that suited him. To attack immortality would be to attack his vested interests. This is the background of Feuerbach's critique of Christianity, primarily the critique of an immortality which was an ideology or a symptom of a degradation of work and the absence of that real community which is the proper environment of the soul and the pledge of an eternal city. It is not misery which should lend force to the idea of heaven, but mundane happiness which points to an eternal happiness. Marx's attack on religion as opium is really an attack on the ideology of the enclosed ego, and is to be traced historically to the nominalist dissolution of society.

Feuerbach was aware that he was driving elements in Luther to their conclusion, but the cultural conditions which are the object of his critique go back equally to Catholic writers. The grand philosophical crystallisation occurs in Descartes.

The *ego sum res cogitans*, I am a thinking being, is the ego of nominalism. It is a substance "requiring nothing beyond itself to be or to be conceived": no social matrix, no historical development, and no body, the body which inserts us in history and in a human community. His philosophy makes an absolute rift between thought and extension, and between the rational principle in man and what was animal in him. The extended and the animal were relegated to the sphere of sheer mechanism, which nevertheless was the object of the *res cogitans* employing a method derived from mathematics. Everything else in the world other than man's rational substance was a mechanism to be understood and used by Western man employing clear and distinct concepts, and stripped of imagination and feeling.

Sympathy with the animal was a product of ignorance. If a dog yelped under vivisection, you could discount it as a mechanical reaction like the chiming of a clock when set. This leaves the animal side of man the absolute object of rational adjustment according to laws which the mathematicised ego discovers. Human behaviour was to fall under a definitive ethic, which Descartes never completed, mathematically certain in its prescriptions. He wished to be certain of his actions with that kind of certainty. In fact one side of man could be exploited by the other, so that the exploitation of nature and the self-exploitation of man here clearly fall together. This is what self-mastery may come to mean.

That we can undertake this kind of self-mastery, that we can undertake to exploit ourselves, that we can formulate a certain rational law to which we must be subject, is a fact of vast importance. It connects with our treatment of nature and of other men. You could not drive the cogs of the machine, nor the machine-minders, without driving yourself, and the picture of the self-made man, or the man who has driven himself to achieve a "rationally" conceived goal, becomes the ideal of a technical society. We turn ourselves into utilities, into objects of use, with which we can get somewhere, whereas there is no meaning and no utility unless man stands above the sphere of use. Otherwise means become ends and, lacking any other reference, become meaningless and suicidal.

If we allow the thin abstract upper stratum of consciousness to dominate all the rest of what we are, if we prefer cute conceptual arrangements to wisdom, we are looking for social and psychological trouble. Thinking and using thought are two quite different operations. Thinking is an end in itself, and then it is a contemplative wisdom. Intellect as means is then no longer the essence of man. It is in the hands of something else. It will in fact become the prey of the dark forces in our nature which it has affected to dominate. The dialectic of Cartesianism and of Puritanism ends in the domination of the animal. The descendant of the Bible Christian becomes the purveyor of porn, after the attempts to suppress it by legislation have failed.

It would be well for us to remember that our conceptual ordering mind, Descartes's *res cogitans* and the seat of our clear and distinct ideas, is like the top of an iceberg supported by a much larger underlying bulk, from which Descartes tried to separate it. Our bodies and instincts have been formed by billions of years of evolutionary experience and, if you like, wisdom, and refuse to toe the line to an upstart new arrival. We are not that of which we are clearly and distinctly aware, and which we know through and through. We are largely unknown to ourselves and have to learn to live with what St Augustine called the abyss of human nature.

If we interfere unwisely with the submerged part of the iceberg, it will be like manipulating external nature with a high hand, and destroying the pre-conscious with bulldozers and insecticides. There is psychological as well as chemical pollution, and the fundamental *yang* attitude behind both is the same. Here again, we must live not on ourselves but with ourselves, or the sub-rational will take revenge on us as it did through Hitler, an inevitable phenomenon of a utilitarian rationalising society and a product of the Enlightenment. The candle of the Lord does ill to forget the subterranean abysses from which its substance was mined.

One finds a particularly explosive *yang* mixture of Puritanism and Cartesian rationalism in Kant, who stands on the threshold of nineteenth-century industrial revolution. In his philosophy the moral or noumenal ego cuts loose from the empirical world and empirical ego, to which it returns to dominate. There is a dualism of the self. On the one hand there is a rational self, the bearer of the pure moral law of duty, which imposes an abstract but iron categorical imperative on the empirical or ordinary natural self. This is the self of inclination, of pleasure and pain, of instincts and impulses, tied up with the natural world and its causal processes, and seeking happiness. This self Kant calls the pathological self, and morality consists in the suppression of the pathological by the pure noumenal self, which is, as it were, the God within us, but subject to no superior divinity because its commands are absolute and unconditional.

Man is autonomous and carries within himself the principle of his own laceration. Caught up as empirical self in the chain of Newtonian time and causality, he must flagellate himself from within, by virtue of having built into him an unremitting and unconditional divine voice. What you have is a modern form of Stoicism, which summons to self-oppression as the essence of moral duty. The Yahweh of the Ten Commandments has come down from Sinai to roost, so that man crushes himself by his own divinity.*
"Be it done unto me" cannot be spoken by the autono-

---

*   See Herbert Tucker, *Philosophy and Myth in Karl Marx*, pp. 33–9.

mous man, and his nemesis is to become the victim of necessity, as happens in Marxism.

This return of divinity upon man was to have a momentous history, through Hegel and Feuerbach to Marx. Roused to indignation by the oppression of man by man, Marx also sees into the divisions within man caused by the idolatry of power and money and illustrates to the point of genius the connection between the inner and the outer oppression. But it is difficult for a critic to escape from what he criticises, and Marx's premises still lie within what I shall call without prejudice the Newtonian order.

His materialism, his determinism, his identification of religion with the ungodly constructions of capitalist moralism, still fall within that narrow and abstract conception of causality which tie the hands of human liberty, and lead, through the rational exploitation of nature as a causal process, to the identification of time with money. *Chronos* remains God whatever other gods you may have overthrown. The universe works. Machines work. Man must work. As Josef Pieper has pointed out, for Kant even philosophy is work. The world of work is the world of subjugation chronometrically ordered, of *yang* attitudes, and this world Marx has never transcended. It is Marxism which has carried abstract causality and its applications to the East, and threatens to overthrow philosophies which know better.

But a world of expanding work and expanding economies, where even feminism has gone *yang*, is working itself to a standstill, and suffocating in its own manly sweat. That phase of Western Christian culture is over. One of the signs of it is the manner in which the young are opting out of work, opting out of money and a work economy, and opting out of a Christianity which they identify with the Cartesian order. The identification is erroneous. It forgets, for instance, St Augustine and his critique of the Manichaeans and Stoics, of whose Kantian attitude to the feelings he says, "who would not say that such insensibility is not worse than sin".

Christianity has reserves of *yin*, and the notion of the Church as the Mother of God will survive the Flight from Woman.* But we seem to be learning some of these things from the East, and the interest of the young in these philosophies is significant.

The notion of renewal, of the bursting of the cerements by some sort of resurrected life, is somewhat of a mystery, as all spontaneous creation is. Our Western Christian culture carries a resurrection in its heart. There are various possible occasions for its reappearance, and one of them seems to me to be contact with Eastern religion and philosophy, and the revival of the idea and practice of contemplation. There is a danger in this, the danger, as Jung so often pointed out, that we may sell our birthright for Oriental ideas, just as the East has sold out so much for our materialism and technology. So many of our generation have tried to go Eastern and made of Kathmandu their Holy Land. This is usually most unwise. We must remem-

---

* The title of a significant book by Karl Stern.

ber that we can never get rid of our past. We may ignore it, despise it, repent of it, but we can never get rid of it.

If, for instance, we ignore or despise it, it will still contain the constructions and the valuations which made it possible for us to take up these attitudes. The ground on which we stand is always holy, and you should not make an Arabian carpet of it which will waft you off to the loss of your roots. We can set out only from where we are. That is one of the profound truisms.

But this is anything but an argument for not taking to heart what we can get from others. The *yang* phase of our culture can find many correctives in Eastern thought, the notions of *yin* and *yang* themselves offering great opportunities of nuancing and subtilising our harshnesses, and balancing our antagonisms. I find the terms on the lips of students where they never were in my generation. But, for many of us at any rate, it would be wiser if these Eastern ideas served to remind us of things that have been forgotten or have gone stale in our own tradition, and brought new life to them. It would be mistaken to look at a Buddha with a lotus in his hand and forget that long ago we heard the advice to consider the lilies of the field and how they grow.

I heard many moral thunderings from the pulpit when I was a boy, but I never saw a preacher who took that advice and, plucking a flower from behind his ear, said, "Let us now consider this veld flower." The thunderings have been somewhat mitigated by the Zen saying that the conflict between right and wrong is a sickness of the mind.

5 : THE YIN AND THE YANG IN CHRISTIAN CULTURE

There is always a black in the white and a white in the black, as Christ saw in the story of the woman taken in adultery, a story which the stock *yin–yang* diagram fits very well. A book like Blythe's *Zen in English Literature* will convince you how much of Zen is already familiar to us.

What we most need reminding of is that we have a contemplative tradition, a tradition of, like Mary, pondering things in our heart, the heart of which Pascal is speaking when he attacks the spirit of geometry in Descartes. The need for contemplation, and the meditative wisdom of the Lady Sophia, is the need for the recovery of the *yin*, for receptive inner growth as against external manipulation and organisation, or the inner manipulation of the Stoic kind. The figure of contemplation has in our tradition always been feminine, be it the Wisdom of the Sapiential books which the Church has appropriated as Mary, or Diotima, who in the *Symposium of Plato* is made to say what Socrates himself will not say directly, or the many figures of Truth in medieval art, or the figure of Beatrice in Dante.

If we have not pondered the significance of this in our hearts, perhaps we did not know that Descartes lost his mother when he was a baby. Perhaps there is nothing which will arouse the contemplative latent in each of us better than the *Tao-te-Ching*, the ancient Chinese classic ascribed to Lao-tzu.

> The spirit of the valley never dies.
> This is called the mysterious woman.
> The gateway of the mysterious woman
> Is called the root of heaven and earth

> Dimly visible, it seems as if it were there,
> Yet use will never drain it. (VI)

> Know the male
> But keep to the role of the female
> And be a ravine to the Empire
> Then the constant virtue will not desert you
> And you will again return to being a babe. (XXVIII)

Which reminds us that we were once told to become as little children, and we forgot the advice and did not meditate on the fact that little children fare badly without a mother. In any event the *Tao-te-Ching*, to which Zen owes so much, is a mystical book which tells us to follow the Tao, leaning back receptively on the wisdom that is inherent in nature, knowing that busy organising both of our lives and of the political set-up defeats its own ends, quieting the manipulative grasping reason, and realising that there is often more wisdom in our bodies formed by the eternal Tao than in our minds. We must learn the wisdom of being stupid, and of resting on a self which is so much more, and so much wiser, than an abstracted pure intellect.

What we require, then, is spontaneity and simplicity, not the simplicity which rests on the absence of thought, not the spontaneity of mere impulse, but an attitude completing a discipline, an *ascesis*, which has become second nature. Like Zen spontaneity Christian spontaneity requires a yoga, a *jugum*, a yoke which we are to bear lightly.

You shoulder your cross and dance with it, but the ponderosity of the cross gives substance to your dance.

Spontaneity, in the actions of Christ or of the Zen masters, is an outflow of wisdom, eternally simple action, action in depth, and not in the linear causal series. Only thus do we rise above *maya*, a word connected etymologically with measuring, thus not merely a world of illusion but a world in which you have everything taped.

If you find it somewhat commonplace to look at a lily of the field – of the field, mark you, not of an organised flower show (you have to go to it) – try looking at a Taoist brush-drawing of a bamboo. It will tell you much the same. It is the only abiding road through the bamboo curtain.

6 : Idealism and Materialism in Ethics

I wish to talk about idealism and materialism at issue with each other. The best service that I can render is to explain that it is no longer an issue. It is not that the problem has been solved one way or the other. That is not the way that things happen in philosophy. Questions get formulated upon a certain background, and then one finds that the background has changed. The assumptions and premises which underlay the formulation of the question have been replaced or undermined, and the questions resting on them lose their significance. They come to be regarded as pseudo-questions. In philosophy we do not so much come up with answers, but with new formulations of the perpetual questioning proper to philosophy.

Let us commence by taking a few bearings on the matter in hand.

The first point that I want to call attention to is that ethics has to do with man as a subject, and not as a thing. We can, of course, treat man as a thing. We can weigh and measure him, discover his chemical composition, or determine his rate of acceleration if he falls out of the window. When we so regard him we do not treat him specifically as a man. Something specifically human, indeed the very point of view from which we make the investigation, has escaped us.

We are apt, however, to play the trick of giving a description of a world of objects, and then assimilating the describer to the description. We account for him in terms of an objective description of things. We then get statements like that of Sir James Jeans when, referring to the vastness of the universe discovered by astronomy, he writes,

> Into such a universe we have stumbled, if not exactly by mistake, at least as the result of what may properly be described as an accident.

The describer has fallen a victim to the description, in terms of which the description itself is an accident ultimately devoid of meaning. Jeans jumps from the physical smallness of man to his insignificance.

Yet it is evident that importance is not relative to size and duration, and that it is from us that the latter acquire significance. We may take it for granted that no nebula, however big, ever felt proud of the fact, and that no pebble, however small, had an inferiority feeling about it. A man can compare himself with other beings, and indeed with the stellar universe itself, and in this respect he is different from any other being of our experience. And that we have experience is the significant fact.

Experience is an interiorisation of the world, and the condition of any exteriorisation of ourselves. Open a man and you will find in him mountains, seas, and stars present in a manner in which we are sure they are not present in a stone or a plant. That is what we mean by saying that he has a mind. In a way, a man is bigger than this universe in the face of which he can make himself feel so small. He can pack its vast spaces into his head. Here we have the essential difference between a man and a stone, namely, that the stone is in the man in a manner in which the man is not in the stone. I can walk from here to there because "there" is already within me, but no stone ever threw itself.

But man does not become physically greater for containing so much. We make great efforts to put a man on the moon, and we neglect the extraordinary phenomenon of the moon in the man, which is the presupposition of our rocketry. If we want to feel swollen-headed, that is the true occasion. But the notions of bigness and smallness do not apply to the mind except metaphorically. When man compares himself with a stone or a star it is by virtue of a power which puts him beyond comparison with them. Similarly he can say that he is in a body and determined by a body because his body is already in him and determined by him.

Furthermore, he contains himself. He is self-conscious. He can say "I", and "I am a man." He does not comprehend himself in the manner in which, nor with the clarity with which, he comprehends a stone. I suppose that it is irritation with this lack of clarity which so often persuades him to alienate himself from himself, and to treat himself as an object. But we have to accept ourselves as subjects, and avoid the mistake of thinking that the world contains two sorts of *things*, subjects and objects. Such a classification would presuppose a classifier which escapes it. We have to accept an ultimate polarity, and it is with the consequences of this that modern philosophy is largely concerned.

I have tried to bring before you the awareness that it is equally true to say that the world is in me, and that I am in the universe. I am going to see myself as a mote of dust whose position and action are entirely the resultants of the forces that surround it. I shall entertain a vision of cosmic determinism. Further, what I see out there is matter, and the sort of determinism at which I shall arrive is a materialist determinism.

Suppose, on the other hand, I lay the emphasis on the fact that the world is in me. Suppose I lay stress on the fact that the idea comes first, and that the pointing to a corresponding object is secondary. I shall very probably, then, be an idealist. I may go further and regard matter as an illusion, or as a precipitate of the idea, or as an objectification wrought by spirit in accordance with its own need. I shall then become an absolute idealist.

I should regard both these positions as erroneous because each loses sight of the wholeness of the initial situation. They are complementary errors, and our philosophy since Descartes has presented the spectacle of two ghosts quarrelling with each other.

Descartes came to the conclusion that he was pure thinking being, and after Descartes every philosopher was bound to make theory of knowledge his central interest. Descartes differed from St Thomas in not regarding the idea as a window, as it were, through which we directly saw reality, but as itself the object and terminus of thought. When we think, we think about ideas. He required a God to enable us to posit a reality independent of the ideas to which they corresponded. There was thus a question of the reality of the world to which the ideas seemed to refer. The unity of mind and body, idea and world, was lost, and consciousness and the world were regarded as two separate realities, which opens the possibility of reducing one to the other.

The idealists emphasised consciousness and gave it a priority. They saw it as something original, self-contained and active. Descartes remained a dualist, and he posited a God to maintain the connection between mind and matter. The tendency of idealism, however, was to eliminate the world as a source of knowledge. Truth is literally something which one excogitates. Perception comes to be regarded as confused knowledge which must be replaced by the clarity of the self-sufficient idea. Consciousness has to return to itself and to overcome its estrangement from itself in matter. It must become a pure for-itself. It must become a consciousness of consciousness, and then we have the culmination of idealism in Hegel.

Empiricism did just the opposite. While idealism had a vision of the spontaneity and activity of the mind, empiricism also had a basic vision, but it was a vision of the passivity of consciousness, its sensitivity to impressions, culminating in the notion of the mind as a *tabula rasa*, a blank sheet on which the outside world impressed itself.

6 : IDEALISM AND MATERIALISM IN ETHICS

The empiricists tried to do justice to the fact that there is an external world which imposes itself on us, and to which we must conform. All knowledge, they said, originated from experience of the world. In the extreme case of Descartes's contemporary, Hobbes, these impressions were quite mechanically caused, and the way in which they were associated and worked up into knowledge followed physical laws of association.

For the empiricist there is such a thing as a world-in-itself, what one might call a brute reality. To some extent this was posited for the purpose of science. The scientist must be an observer. He must achieve objectivity. He must see the world "as it is" without subjective interference. This world which is spread out before us is simply *there*. It is in itself and must be made to speak for itself.

One arrives, then, at two mutually conflicting positions, the world as the creation or even the dream of mind; and on the other hand the mind as the product or accident or epiphenomenon of matter, even as the bad dream of matter. On their premises the argument between the two parties cannot possibly be concluded. It can go on for ever. This ought to lead one to suspect that the question, "Idealism or materialism?", is a pseudo-question, and that the only way to deal with it is to burke it. And that is what modern philosophy has done.

Let us try to look quite simply at the facts of the case. Here is a brown table before me. I know perfectly well that I am not the table. I am here and the table is there. We should notice that the thereness of the table is relative to my hereness. Thereness is not a quality of the table independent of me. It is my presence that puts it there. The whole world is there because I put it there. It is I who object the table and the world. Object is a purely correlative term. It is I who make the world to exist as something *there*. Hence to try to give an account of myself purely in terms of the *there*, as the materialist or the determinist does, is simply to forget the initial act by which the *there* is there at all. On the other hand I did not descend preformed from heaven to give thereness to the table. If there is no object without the presence of consciousness, so there is no consciousness without an object. Man is always man in the world, while the very notion of world implies a human subject.

Let us come back to the table. I say, "The table is brown." I can raise all sorts of puzzles about this. I know that I am perceiving the table by means of a complicated physiological mechanism. There is something out there which affects my sense organs and I see the object as brown. But brownness is in a sense a human phenomenon. It is an appearance of something to me. I can raise the question whether the table "in itself" is really brown, or whether its brownness is something which is "merely subjective", a sort of psychological paint with which I have covered the table.

As long as I fail to think in terms of the notion of man-in-the-world, the problem is quite insoluble. It is stated so as to have no solution. I am trying to solve a problem which involves subjectivity by reducing both the thing seen and the seeing thing to a complex of physiological mechanisms, to objects, whereas the problem is the relation of a subject to an object, of a *thing*, to what is not properly speaking a thing at all. The question whether the brownness of the table is independent of my perceptual processes makes no sense at all. Unseen colours like unheard sounds are in a way nonsensical phrases. Of course sounds and colours occur which I do not hear or see, but the very conception of colour and sound involves the presence of a sentient subject.

The table is brown as a constituent of the world, but the world is there as correlative to a subject. The table is really brown, but it is really there because there is a really here in relation to whose projects it is a table at all. Nothing exists in isolation. The world is a society, and things are what they are only in relation to other things. The table is neither objectively nor subjectively brown; but brown in a society which includes subjects.

As a consequence of this way of looking at things, not only do the old puzzles of idealism versus materialism disappear, but so do those of absolute freedom versus determinism, and subjectivism versus objectivism. They represent types of reductionism based on the Cartesian reduction of reality to absolute spirit and absolute matter, in terms of one of which we then endeavour to render the other. Take the instance of absolute determinism. We ob-ject a world of causally connected events, and then ignoring the process by which it has been objected – the activity of a subject which by that activity shows itself not to be a thing

– we try to reduce the subject to a thing by assimilating it to the world which has been objected, reducing the here to the there. We thus alienate ourselves from ourselves and make nonsense of the whole process.

Absolute libertarianism makes the same mistake in reverse. It fails to see that the subject exists only as intention upon the world. Man himself is the source of his actions but he himself as being-in-the-world is a facticity which sets limits, without which his action has neither roots in nor relevance to the world. There is no thinking without language in which our thought is cast, no philosophy without the influence of tradition, no personal religion without institutions, no emotional life without the influence of the family and inherited temperamental make-up. But these influences are, as it were, recreated in us, and are rather things which we use than are used by. To think that we are used by them is anthropomorphic thinking, since the relation of use is not a relation of *things*, but of subjects to things.

There is a certain consensus in modern thought that the primary datum of philosophy is existence, and that existence cannot be broken down into a dichotomy of spirit and matter. We cannot think the subject and the world as separate from each other. Neither can we reduce the subject to a Cartesian "I think". For in the first place my body is the means by which I am present in the world, and which bears witness to my biological bond with others; and secondly by virtue of the social character of language and its close connection with thought, the "I think" is always in a sense a "We think". This table is something at which I *sit*, something made and used, something picked out from the surroundings by the common word "table", and following certain social conventions of structure.

Hence what we endeavour to do, at any rate in our philosophical generation, is to give expression to the fact that existence is an *encounter* between subjects and the world, that neither term in the encounter has meaning without the other. Another way of expressing it is to say that existence is a dialogue. That is to say that the unity of subject and the world is a dialectical unity. This conversation of man with the world takes place in time and history. It is expressed in the labour by which existence is transformed. Thus existence is conceived of as a temporality which is a progressive process of the humanisation of the world.

Time is not the abstract and neutral framework of events, as conceived by Newton, but relates to a subject who constitutes a "now" by his presence to the world. For what do we mean when we say that one event occurs *after* another? There can be no conception of "after" unless what precedes it is held in the presence of a subject. Somehow, what went before must be held onto. Physically, the past has gone, but it is recreated by us and placed before what is now present to us. Unless the past is held onto there can be no conception of a succession. There is no time without memory. Further, we do not remember at random, but what we remember is organised in the light of the projects which we entertain for the future. If there is no time without memory, neither is there time without anticipation.

In short, there is no time without subjectivity; and objectivism, the attempt to ascribe qualities to the world in abstraction from a subject, can form no idea of time. In this sense the idea of history is prior to the idea of physical time. History can be thought of as located in an inhuman physical time only by forgetting the process by which the latter concept was formed, thereby failing to see that it is an abstraction formed in, by, and for a community of men engaged in the realisation of meaning in the world. I pointed out earlier that if man was in space, space was also in man. This is true also of time, and we can make a cognate series of mistakes by forgetting to hold both truths together in the concept of existence as a dialectic.

We can say, then, that the Cartesian "I think ideas", which I excogitate from the essence of a thinking substance, has given place to "We construct a world", thinking it by means of a language which has been communally and historically formed, and which elicits from us in the process of its historical humanisation the meaning of our subjectivity and of our presence here. For we should remember that the idea of existence involves not simply the co-presence of the individual subject and the world, but the co-presence and immediate availability to each other of subjects. Men are not self-enclosed atoms of consciousness, but are given in a social togetherness, the forms of which influence their interpretation of the cosmos.

The intelligibility of the world and the intelligibility of

6 : IDEALISM AND MATERIALISM IN ETHICS

the social order in which we live are closely linked. The efforts which we make to understand the world, for instance in the forms of science which we cultivate, are relative to our social projects, just as our society must be realistically true to an objective order of things revealed by our thought. Any anthropologist will demonstrate the connection between social structures and cosmologies. Any reformer wishing to introduce modern science and techniques to primitive nations knows that he must teach that society to want more or less the same things as the societies which evolved that science, and to develop institutions which express those projects.

The subject of science is a "we", and if that "we" does not make sense, the science will in the long run not make sense either. Insofar as religion and morality are necessary to make sense of the "we", they are a prerequisite of the intelligibility of science, as Plato long ago pointed out in his argument for the primacy of the form of the Good. Science remains a human and social activity, in spite of the temptation which it has put into our hands to reduce the whole furniture of heaven and earth to "things", to be related in an "objective" and "impersonal" way.

We should notice that the climate of opinion here sketched is not favourable to the continuation of the great revolutions which have rent the modern world. A revolution is essentially an attempt to break with history, and the recovery of the notion of the primacy of historical time has overcome the dehistorising and de-socialising of the thinking subject by Cartesianism. Both idealism and materialism contributed to the revolutionary atmosphere. The emphasis on the subject as activity, forming rather than formed by the world, gives licence to the ideal of shattering the outer world, including the social order, in order to mould it nearer to the heart's desire. It is the function of man to dominate the outer order rather than, as Burke argued, to lie open to the *logos* and experience enshrined in it.

Man may impose himself on past and future generations either by right of the promptings of the heart or by right of the deliveries of a reason which is reduced to a logical manipulation of ideas. The materialist, too, has his romantic dreams, but, realising that to dominate nature we must understand it, he builds up a picture of the progress of nature and history as a juggernaut to whose imperious demands the persuasions of tradition, and the niceties of humane consideration, should not be allowed to impose a barrier. He imposes the realm of the so-called objective in a manner equally shattering to the existence which is slowly built up by the inseparable marriage of man and the world.

The rationalist, the Rousseauist sentimentalist and the Marxist revolutionist are all birds of a feather, born of the dichotomy of man and the world, and inadequate to an era where the "we" is a more pressing fact than ever, and where we must use science not to dominate men and rape nature, but to secure a cooperation dictated by a day-to-day sensitivity to a changing world. We have to develop a dialectic which is not geared to the idea of violence, but to the project of realising the human possibilities given in our facticity, a project which does not require world revolution but the realisation of the possibilities given in various local situations. Hence constructive pluralism, rather than a uniform world revolutionary industrialism, seems to be what contemporary ethics demands.

Contemporary ethics, then, contrasts relativity and relativism, subjectivity and subjectivism, objectivity and objectivism, materiality and materialism, and *hoc genus omne*. To realise the relativity of our knowledge as time-bound and historical is a very different thing from constructing a relativism which we hold to be true for all time. To hold that an object is an object only for a subject is a very different thing from holding that, in that relation, the object is not revealed, and that knowledge will be infected with the merely personal if we do not succeed in bracketing the subject. On the whole there is an impatience with systems, including those of idealism and materialism, on the grounds that systems are in the nature of the case abstractions which get between us and the concrete reality.

Recently a young man came to see me because he could not see over the rim of a total determinism. The theory had totally occluded the patent fact that he had taken the initiative of coming to see me. I did not put up a counter-theory, but called his attention to the fact of his coming through the door, being accepted by me as a person and not as a thing or a concept, and to the improbability of the chair ever walking out through the door. We can imprison ourselves in systems and ideologies which turn ourselves and the world into ghosts of themselves, and the result of philosophy should not so much be to put us in possession of coherent systems of ideas as to enable us to accept ourselves and the things, events and situations about us in what a Zen Buddhist would call their suchness. Many modern philosophers have been sympathetic to Zen because of its attempt to free us from the grid of interpretations which prevent our seeing things with a single eye and encountering reality with a childlike directness.

This endeavour to let essences, as they fall within our creative relationship to the world, speak for themselves, is called phenomenology. It is a long word, but it simply indicates a return to the single eye. It is an endeavour to describe what appears to us directly as it appears, without preconceptions and without presuppositions. Thus we do not approach a phenomenon like love with a system like that of idealism or materialism, by assimilation to which we seek to render it intelligible, but simply take love as it appears in fact and try to let it speak out its own essence. We do not take it as a psychological fact or a physiological fact or any other *kind* of fact, because that is already to impose an abstraction upon it.

The procedure is not new. You know the story of the woman taken in adultery. The Pharisees approached the case with an interpretative system: there is a category of crime called adultery for which the penalty is stoning. What Christ brings home to them is that they are alienated from themselves, and that they are hiding their personal guilt from themselves behind this system. His own attitude to the adultery of the woman is not permissive. He destroys the adulteress within her, whereas the Pharisees would not have expunged the adultery but only the body of the adulteress. Christ does not substitute another set of principles for the Pharisaic law. He rises above all principles to the reality directly revealed in his relation to the woman, and does something to her.

It is not the function of the moral philosopher to judge in the light of some system or set of principles, idealistic or otherwise. It is never the function of a good man to judge. He has to enter into a dialogue with the moral situation, as Christ did with the woman, and creatively bring out of it some contribution to the great dialogue of man with man, and man with the world, which elicits the meaning of history. There are more things in good and evil than are dreamt of in our philosophy.

When one meditates upon this action of Christ one is impressed by its spontaneity. There is no appeal to a principle like, duty must be done, or, the aim of human action is the maximisation of pleasure, or to reasons for the wrongness of adultery. His action comes directly out of what he is, and from the immediate encounter.

Jung is referring to this immediacy of encounter when he says,

> If the doctor wants to offer guidance to another ... he must be in touch with this other person's psychic life. He is never in touch when he passes judgement. Whether he puts his judgements into words, or keeps

> them to himself makes not the slightest difference ... If the doctor wishes to help a human being he must be able to accept him as he is. And he can do this in reality only when he has already seen and accepted himself as he is.
>
> (MODERN MAN IN SEARCH OF A SOUL, PP. 270–1)

That is, he must immediately encounter himself, not be hidden from himself by norms or ideals or pictures of himself. That is the essence of spontaneity.

We are probably right in being suspicious of the pretensions of moralists, and of a great deal of what passes for morality. Much of morality arises from disreputable reasons – resentment, revenge, pusillanimity, fear, egocentricity – and one can appreciate why Nietzsche wanted to make a clean sweep of it. He, too, was in search of spontaneity, but whether his vitalism, or that of D.H. Lawrence, is the end of the search is a further question. It is true that it does some justice to the fact that we often do better on instinct than on a reasoned theory.

> There are times when men's passions are much more trustworthy than their principles. Since opposed principles, or ideologies, are irreconcilable, wars fought over principle will be wars of mutual annihilation. But wars fought for simple greed will be far less destructive, because the aggressor will be careful not to destroy what he is fighting to capture. Reasonable men will always be capable of compromise, but men who have dehumanised themselves by becoming the blind worship-

pers of an idea or an ideal are fanatics whose devotion to abstractions makes them the enemies of life.
(WATTS, *THE WAY OF ZEN*, PP. 29–30)

One of the main problems of the ethical life is to escape from an abstract or contrived persona acting on abstract principles in order to opt out of one's essential humanity, out of the original being which is ontologically in union with things and other people.

> Our problem is that the power of thought enables us to construct symbols of things apart from the things themselves. This includes the ability to make a symbol, an idea of ourselves apart from ourselves. Because the idea is so much more comprehensible than the reality, the symbol so much more stable than the fact, we learn to identify ourselves with our idea of ourselves. Hence the subjective feeling of a 'self' which 'has' a mind, of an inwardly isolated subject to whom experiences involuntarily happen.
> (WATTS, PP. 119–20)

We "style" ourselves on the advertisements that we read or on books or films, we picture ourselves as old or retired, or honoured, as professors or Pharisees or businessmen, and proceed to act according to the idea, that is, according to a "me" which may quite overlay the original "I", which can be projected only by idealisation into past and future; and to this idealisation we fit our ideas of right and wrong. Most of our ideas of right and wrong are relative to a pseudo-self, e.g. a Pharisaical self, whereas we should act directly out of what we are and not out of what we were or want to be or fear to be. Hence the lines in the oldest Zen poem (quoted by Watts, p.165):

> If you want to get the plain truth
> Be not concerned with right and wrong.
> The conflict between right and wrong
> Is the sickness of the mind.

We can connect this with the Confucian principle that "it is man who makes truth great, not truth which makes man great". Hence the Confucian emphasis on *jen*, or humanness, which is rooted in the concrete or true self against which we must correct our symbolisings and abstractions. This Confucian true self is not the isolated Cartesian individual, but a self which is directly aware of its solidarity with other men and with nature, so that its Taoist scepticism with respect to artificial right and wrong is precisely what lays the foundations of morality. Hence to say that it is man who makes truth great is precisely also what removes truth from the sphere of a subjectivism or relativism. Man is greater than the construct which he makes of himself, and he has to brush away the construct and act out of original nature. Good action is unselfconscious. Moral ideals are the curse of morality.

The central problem of the moral judgement thus becomes the problem of spontaneity, and on this there is a certain coincidence of witness from the Christian and Oriental traditions, and the modern existentialist. In all

6 : IDEALISM AND MATERIALISM IN ETHICS

these positions the fact of what would nowadays be called encounter is central, and the solidarity of man with his fellows and with nature. Being is revealed in human being, and spontaneity then becomes not the quirk of the isolated individual but an expression or discovery of reality. It is an act of constructing a common world which is deformed and fragmented by actions proceeding from the abstract ego. This deformation is the construction of what a Buddhist would call *samsara*.

"The soul", as Goldbrunner puts it, referring to the position of modern philosophy (*Cure of Mind and Cure of Soul*, p. 35),

> is no longer 'world-less', it is at home in the world and for its self-realisation it looks not merely to the process in the interior sphere, and the integration of consciousness and the unconscious, but also the integration of itself and the world; i.e. action is required if it is to become itself. Decision within and action without both form part of the basic structure of existence.

Perhaps this is all summed up in the famous dictum of St Augustine: *ama et fac quod vis*. This would be a principle of anarchy if the love which he intends were merely a private emotion. But for St Augustine love is a self-transcending principle. It is that by which we go out to the objective and concrete. As St Thomas puts it, by the intellect we seek abstractions, but love is not satisfied with anything less than the thing itself. It is, when genuine, not an act by which we cut things down to our own size, but by which we abandon ourselves to the demands of the thing loved. In that sense it is self-less. It asserts the human instead of the merely "me". *Ama* then means, find your true humanity (*jen*), which is there only as a genuine reciprocity with God, your fellow men, and nature, and *act* accordingly: *fac* quod *vis*.

To act is thus not merely to suffer or be determined by the world, not to dictate to it, but to humanise a world which is *there*, with all its exigencies and all its possibilities, only by an act of love. Morality then means the discovery and construction of the world in company with one's fellows, and not a set of prohibitions and abstractions relative to our egoisms. The Buddhist critique of the finite self and its injunction, "Do not seek the truth, only avoid opinions," are thus seen to stand in the closest connection with each other. The "me" and the abstractions with which it buttresses itself are only opinions. Every man is naturally in the truth – a Zenist would say that he is a Buddha; a Christian, that he is in the image of God – and spontaneity is to act out the truth which is concealed by division and opinion.

What has all this to do with my original theme of idealism and materialism? Perhaps simply that they are both opinions, and that the realities of the moral life cut deeper than both. They are both dangerous opinions in that they rest on a radical separation of man and the world, each in their way finally reducing one to the other. We end up with the sense either of having the world in our grip or of being in the grip of the world, of thinking that we are God or of thinking that we are pawns, and perhaps these two forms of consciousness have a basic similarity and a common despair.

Philosophy is a dangerous occupation, and one is always in danger of mistaking its constructions for reality. It may, of course, be retorted that in this chapter I have been theorising myself, and simply putting up an alternative construction. I could reply in the words of a Buddhist that Buddhism was using a thorn to take out a thorn, after which one throws both away. It is useless to use blood to wash away blood, and what I have tried to do is to point at the moral fact rather than explain it. It remains a mystery to me. If I have called your attention to yourselves you can forget about me.

In conclusion, then, it must not be thought that this question of materialism and idealism is only for the philosophy lecture theatre. When Descartes declared that we can know only our ideas, he was in fact proclaiming the death of the medieval world in which St Thomas had said that we directly know being through ideas. Descartes summoned God to guarantee the coincidence of our ideas with the reality which they seemed to represent. But in fact this was the beginning of the dismissal of God.

St Thomas says in the *De Veritate* that the human mind is measured by natural things. It must conform to an independent nature, a nature in the image of God, whose independence is guaranteed by the act of creation. And because God is the *creator omnium* his mind is the *mensurans* of all things, and by no means *mensurata*. It is the intelligence of God which gives being to things, and hence he knows them in his creative ideas. But the Cartesian knowledge which knows things in our ideas of them is not itself *mensurata* but has taken the step to self-apotheosis, and to a godlike control of nature.

As I wrote in *The Nature of Philosophical Enquiry* (p. 86): The unity between Descartes's theory of knowledge and his practical intentions is to be found in the conception of instrumentality. Thought is something which we must use, and we cannot use it unless it is in our own power rather than in the power of things. Consequently, nature for the Cartesian must be regarded primarily from the point of view of what we want it to be. In order that it should correspond with human thought and intention it must be *made* to correspond with them. In the last analysis, it is will which constitutes reality to be what it is. Becoming masters and possessors of nature thus involves the project of constructing nature in our own image by means of thought, manipulated according to scientific method.

It is this direction in Descartes which points straight to Hegel. When Hegel says that what is real is what is rational, he is not subjecting the mind to the intrinsic rationality of nature, but on the contrary setting the mind to construct a nature out of its own rationality. This is carrying self-apotheosis a step further. Descartes has not ceased to think in the light of the Christian God, though in the ontological argument for God's existence he is by implication raising his idea of God to the level of the divine self-knowledge, because the argument requires a knowledge of the essence of God.

Marx does not escape the Hegelian self-apotheosis any more than he escapes its idealism. Man is to control history, and the divine providence is otiose. A reality which does not correspond to the dialectic is epiphenomenal, a play of false consciousness. What is, is what I can do. Marx may substitute for the idealist priority of consciousness the materialist priority of economics, but the acceptance of any man-made priority is still to put the key to reality in human hands, hands which will now proceed to construct a Utopia liberated from the disciplines of objective reality, and in fact enslaving man to the will to power, because his mind is *mensurans* and never measured by a history which is not ideal.

Here we have another illustration of the manner in which idealism and materialism reveal themselves as two sides of the same coin. It also reveals a motive for the Marxist attack on existentialism, namely that it undercuts an opposition which is the lifeblood of Marxism, and negates the futurism of a Utopia by the aid of which we dream up a world rising out of the ruins of history and constituted by the heart's desire. If the real is the rational, then what is, is what can be thought and desired. The so-called realism of communism is in fact an unbounded romanticism. All this rests upon the statement in *The Phenomenology of*

Mind that "truth finds the medium of its existence in notions or conceptions alone", which is not so far from the Cartesian position that the objects of knowledge are ideas.

Sartre's flirtation with communism is rooted in a stale rationalism, which corrupts his existentialism with the philosophy of the *philosophes*. His proofs of the non-existence of God from human autonomy are stale, flat and unprofitable, and rest upon a condition of mind which is thoroughly out of date.

In contemporary philosophy we have transcended the conflict between idealism and materialism which has governed Western philosophy for three centuries, and which is rooted in a dualism which separated man and nature. But this is only to go back to the perennial philosophy for which self and not-self mutually support each other. This brings us also a greater understanding of Oriental thought and, for instance, to the Buddhist and Zen insight that every man lives in the world which he is or deserves.

7 : The Human Vision

Since the time of Emmanuel Kant a great deal of emphasis has been placed on the contribution of subjective factors in the constitution of our experience. According to his philosophy, both sensuous and intellectual experience are activities, and activities determined by the innate constructive powers which inhere in human nature. All of us bring to experience a point of view which is, in the first place, that of human nature. Since Kant wrote there has been an enormous elaboration of the idea that the situation and activity of the observer enters into the statement of the observation.

I need only remind you of the part it plays in the statement of the indeterminacy principle in physics, but it has also entered very deeply into the sciences of man. I notice, for instance, that that eminent ancient-historian M. Henri Marrou, admitting a debt to Kant, has attacked nineteenth-century ideas of objectivity and has made a powerful plea for the admission of subjective factors in the reconstitution of the past, affirming, in his own field, the Kantian paradox that you cannot be objective without some degree of subjectivity. He writes:

> The best historian of a man or of an epoch is one who, by his mental disposition and his own human experience, is most closely and intimately related to the spirit

which once animated his hero or heroes. One cannot look for a completely satisfactory biography of Voltaire from a Catholic historian. On the other hand, I have always deplored the fact that the first and greatest historian of the Late Empire was that Voltairean, Gibbon. How could a man of the eighteenth century such as he, so totally out of sympathy with the Christian ideal (religion and barbarism are synonymous in his eyes) 'understand' the civilisation, so profoundly religious in inspiration, that was the Roman Empire after Constantine?
(CROSS CURRENTS, XI, 1, P. 72)

I have quoted from Marrou because he displays a sense of the relevance of the historical situation of the historian to his power of perceiving things. Kant has inherited from Descartes a considerable failure to appreciate the effects of his historical situation upon the philosopher's power of seeing things. The reason for this seems to be that a historian is constantly dealing with the fact of personality, while many philosophers saddle their thought with the abstraction: human nature. Now, human nature is the same in the thirteenth as in the twentieth century, and in Cape Town as in Peking. But no two human personalities are the same. Our personalities are what we make of our natures in the situation in which each of us finds himself, using situation to include historical, geographical, social, inherited biological and other factors.

We perceive things not only from the general point of

view of human nature, but from the particular point of view from which each of us as a person is. That is to say, man in a situation is the perspective from which things are perceived, and he corrects his perceptions according to his knowledge of what and where he is. Thus Marrou exacts self-knowledge from the historian as a *sine qua non* of his writing scientific history. Personal integrity in the widest sense is not an unnecessary requirement in anybody who practises the humane arts and sciences. He cannot perceive truly without it.

Let me mention that Kant is not the only thinker to draw attention to subjective elements in knowledge. It was done, as I think, better, by St Thomas Aquinas, who uses a famous formula, *cognitum est in cognoscente per modum cognoscentis*, the thing known is in the knower, according to the knower's way of existing. I will not trouble you with the technical explication of this formula except to point out that it is more modern than Kant's in the sense that it draws attention not only to the knower's way of thinking but to his way of existing. Aquinas must be taken to mean that the knower perceives the thing known according to his situation as an individual person. Nobody short of the modern existentialists has brought this out better than John Henry Newman.

"Each of two men," he writes in the *Grammar of Assent*, "has a vested interest in all that he himself is; and, moreover, what seems to be common in the two, becomes in fact so uncommon, so *sui simile*, in their respective individualities – the bodily frame of each is so singled out from all other bodies by its special constitution, sound or weak, by its vitality, activity, pathological history and changes, and, again, the mind of each is so distinct from all other minds, in disposition, power, and habits – that instead of saying, as logicians say, that the two differ only in number, we ought, I repeat, rather to say that they differ from each other in all that they are, in identity, in incommunicability, in personality."

If I may take the example of architecture to make my point, let me put it this way. Things are perceived from the standpoint of the individual person existing in history. Now, personality is an existential concept. A person is a total concrete human being. A man's personality includes his body and its quirks by which he is situated in space and time. To say, therefore, that things are perceived from the point of view of the person is to say that they are perceived by the whole man, and to refuse to separate his sensuous from his intellectual perception. Sense experience is for a human being also an intellectual experience witnessing to the real unity of body and soul. If one looks at a building, one is not only receiving certain sense-impressions but assimilating the thing seen into the interpretative system of a definite person. One sees and thinks it at the same time and in a unitary act in which sense and thought are interfused. Similarly when one designs a building, one is performing an autobiographical act. One is saying how one interprets the times, and one's own time. A building has personality to the extent that both body and mind have gone into it. You situate a thing correctly according as you have situated yourself correctly. A good building reflects the human organism taken as a historical fact.

Were one to endeavour to illustrate this, one could best use the structure of a Gothic cathedral. It is related, in its structure and in its purpose, to a body hanging on a cross. The event which it serves, and from which it derives, is in a profound sense historical. It marks a crisis in, and a new beginning of time. It has been prepared for since the Creation, it terminates the loss of humanity through sin, and it opens the time from the Resurrection to the last things. The Church, in the thought of the theology which built the medieval churches, is regarded as the Body of Christ, in which all the faithful are incorporated as members, in the Pauline image, of higher and lower degree, to form one corporate whole which is moving through time in eternity.

The Gothic cathedral, taken as building, incorporates this theology. It arouses an organic and visceral as well as a cerebral response. Its lines sweep us to the infinity which is promised by the Resurrected Body. It grows through time, and is patient of the work of many hands. In the elaboration of its detail it organises and assimilates the multiplicity of the world into a coherent whole. As we can see from the accounts of the building of Chartres, it was able to receive the contribution of all, and to raise the meanest workman to a new power of himself by virtue of its all-embracing plan.

As the Church could make all men members of the

body of Christ, so the building which was to house the real presence could receive the variety of their contribution. It made a real democracy perceptible. It was tolerant of the sculptures both of saints and of sinners, which bear, in their sculptural quality, a relation to the building analogous to that of Greek sculpture to the Parthenon. They are unlike in that they are not idealisations of human nature, but persons who have done well or ill in their time, and have meaning in the procession of creatures, which is the temporal distension of the eternal Body of Christ. Time is not to be swept away, but assumed into the infinity to which all perspectives point.

If one "sees" a Gothic cathedral, this is what one has to see. But one may note how ambiguous the word "seeing" is. You can no more dissociate the physical from the mental seeing than you can dissociate the operations of body and mind in thought. You can bring both organic and spiritual blindness to a perception. As an example of the latter, and to illustrate my point of the all-comprising character of perception, let me quote two examples of "enlightened" perception of the Gothic, the first from David Hume, and the second from Descartes.

Very early in his career Hume wrote an essay to show the absurdity of chivalry, and the tastelessness of those mistresses who are as necessary to a knight "as a God or Saint to a Devotee". He is in fact attacking "barbarism and religion".

> What kind of monstrous Birth this of Chivalry must prove we may learn from considering the different Revolu-

tions in the Arts, particularly in Architecture, and comparing the Gothic with the Grecian Models of it. The one are plain, simple, regular, but withal majestic and beautyful, which when these Barbarians unskillfully imitated, they run into a wild profusion of ornaments, and by their rude Embellishments departed far from Nature and a just Simplicity. They were struck with the Beauties of the ancient Buildings, but ignorant how to preserve a just Mean; and giving an unbounded Liberty to their Fancy in heaping Ornament upon Ornament, they made the whole a heap of Confusion and Irregularity.

One notices a kind of physical disgust for these barbaric structures arising from a disappointed sense of order. One suspects that the Gothic was too close to the earth and the human body to please David Hume. A citizen of the Edinburgh of his time would be sensitive to its smells. Perhaps the root of the matter is that no philosophy is more inimical to the concept of personality than that of Hume.

His greatest work is a treatise of human *nature*, and we are to arrive at human nature by discovering general laws which express necessities of behaviour which are independent of time and place. The historical becomes intelligible only from the viewpoint of an abstract and timeless generality. Simplicity for Hume means generality, the intellectual tidying-up of the hurly-burly of fact, which leads to a Platonic kind of perception which would find more satisfaction in the Parthenon than in Chartres. The world of history is a wild profusion of ornaments which a man of taste and science will not accept as the book of his salvation, but will strip to those general principles which will enable him to control it in accordance with his enlightened sensibilities.

What one is observing in fact is a change of perception which prefers the organised to the organic. I have said sufficient to suggest that there is a connection between the manner in which a particular age perceives the human body and that in which it perceives a building. The Middle Ages were very ignorant of physiology, but they had grasped the truth that the body is an integral part of the person, and that he is related through it to history. Its religion gave due weight to bodily things, and to those sacraments which incorporated him in a mystical body which bore his destinies through history.

The new physiology, at any rate among the Cartesians, abstracted the body from the mind and from history. It isolated it as a system of interacting material parts, and used the machine as a model for the interpretation of its operations. The physiology of Descartes is closely related to his remarkable insensitivity to the importance of history and tradition, and his attachment to the structures which clock-time enables us to investigate and to raise. Organic growth must give way to planning, and he envisaged a science of medicine which would overcome the organic rhythm of birth, maturation and death, and give us bodies with the immortality of a well-run machine.

Look at a Gothic play like *Measure for Measure*, with its charitable estimate of the vitality of the organic, and its acceptance of death and mutability, and remember the part played in it by Angelo, who in his inhuman, "angelic", inorganic fleshlessness – he "pisses ice" – endeavours to impose an abstract puritanical law on the human actuality, and you will appreciate that the age was acutely aware of the clashes in its perceptions. The Duke moves through it like a Providence, not imposing but obeying a law which through the vicissitudes of its operation raises the stainless virgin to a throne. Has it been sufficiently observed that Shakespeare's defence of bawdy raises a monument to Notre Dame?

With this sort of thing in mind, let us recall Descartes's famous record of his perception of the Gothic in *Discours* II. Of his thoughts, he says,

> ... one of the very first that occurred to me was, that there is seldom so much perfection in works composed of many parts, upon which different hands have been employed, as in those completed by a single master. Thus it is observable that the buildings which a single architect has planned and executed, are generally more elegant and commodious than those which several have attempted to improve, by making old walls serve for purposes for which they were not originally built. Thus also, those ancient cities which, from being at first only villages, have become, in course of time, large towns, are usually but ill laid out compared with the regularly constructed towns which a professional ar-

> chitect has freely planted on an open plain; so that although the several buildings of the former may often equal or surpass in beauty those of the latter, yet when one observes their indiscriminate juxtaposition, there a large one and here a small, and the consequent crookedness and irregularity of the streets, one is disposed to allege that chance rather than any human will guided by reason, must have led to such an arrangement.

He goes on to attack the adequacy of a legal system which has slowly evolved from customary law, and to express a preference for a legal code which is the work of a single enlightened lawgiver.

What you have here is an aesthetic and moral perception whose quality is given to it by an inner and subjective world dominated by the idea of abstract law, and by the will to impose mathematical patterns upon nature. It is what I might call authoritarian perception whose sensibilities are mediated by the notion of abstract order. There is to be one method, one science, one scientist, one lawgiver, who is to *dominate* the material, given in time and history, from the point of view of an intellect which has cut itself loose from body, sense, and imagination, in order to make matter and history conform to pure intellect. *Les femmes savantes* will give the tone to society rather than those ladies who have risen from the disordered Gothic imagination of Don Quixote. Unfortunately, with the latter would disappear the Isabellas and Hermiones, who if they were chaste were also usable, which is what a good town and a good building ought to be. You need a geometrical layout to rape a town with traffic and, if you are to choose between a bawd and a Platonist, there is something to be said for Shakespeare's way.

In concluding, I notice that, while I set out to make the general point that sensuous and intellectual perception are inseparable, that we cannot separate body and mind in "seeing" things, and that our seeing will depend on the sort of personality which we bring to it, I have also expressed a preference for the organic over the organisational. But in fact these two points are quite inseparable. One cannot separate the achievement of integrity, the welding into a whole of all one's psychophysical powers, from the act of integrating oneself with one's contemporaries and with history and tradition. A person is private in proportion as he is public, and one wishes to communicate what one sees well because one knows that one is seeing it for everybody. The perceptive man sees something for the human race, and it follows with a necessary logic that to see thus is to see organically.

Chesterton put the question whether dons saw double because they got drunk, or got drunk because they saw double. Undoubtedly, the latter explanation is correct. To be divided in oneself is to have double and conflicting images of things. To divorce the sensuous and the intellectual, body and mind, self and other, the traditional and the new is to forfeit the single eye. It is appalling how many buildings squint. If I have displayed some love of the Gothic it is because the Gothic was contemporary. This does not mean merely that it was of its time. All buildings are of their time. It is very elementary metaphysics that a building which you put up in 1978 is not put up in 1979. It was contemporary because it had inserted calendar time into eternity, and knew where man stood and how he was situated. If you like, it was a historical period in which it was possible to be contemporary because it flowed from a culture which had achieved some wholeness and integrity.

Strictly speaking, it is not all periods which can achieve a contemporary vision. It is a qualitative, not a quantitative concept. If you like, all artists are contemporary but some are more contemporary than others. One's intense dislike of neo-Gothic architecture arises from the perception that the most Gothic building today would be the most modern. Since time is nothing but a growing old, there is nothing new except eternity, and there is no eternity for us but in the now. In fact, nothing is more difficult to achieve than a contemporary perception of things. The recipe for good designing, as for good writing, sounds very simple: be yourself, where you are, now. But we are all running away from time and death, and none of us is himself now. To the extent that the modern world does not know what to do with time, it cannot solve the problem of what to do with space, and the architect who can see space truly will earn our eternal gratitude.

8 : On Justice and Human Rights

Justice is the concern of the political philosopher, of the lawyer, and of the moral philosopher. It is the second of the four cardinal virtues, and it must be connected with its metaphysical roots in the nature of man. The moral virtues are habits by which man actualises his essence, or realises his humanity. Given the perennial view that man is made for truth, then justice is intelligible only when related to this realisation. This is the foundation of natural law theory which relates law, through morality, to the structure of human being. If man has rights it is by virtue of what, ultimately, he is. Justice is that virtue by which we habitually give to every man his due or right, and I wish to relate this giving to the notion of truth, which is a correspondence of man with what he is and with his world, a world whose maturation is its history.

Justice is something proper to the sphere of human existence, and we can extend the notion of just-dealing only analogously to our relations with the subhuman world. We do justice to the subhuman world only by doing justice to men, an action by which we vicariously bring out what is dumb and incompleted in the subhuman world. A right relation to our fellow men involves a right relationship to the subhuman world, exploitation in the one sphere always involving abuse in the other. Human beings are capable of owning things in a manner which is *sui generis*. Man can have belongings, not necessarily material belongings only, to which we say that he has a right, and which we may not take or withhold from him without committing an injustice.

This raises the question of what in fact is due to man, and the still deeper question of how anything at all comes to belong to him, something which may belong to him so deeply that Aristotle can say that our greatest troubles arise from lack of the habit of according it to him. St Thomas Aquinas puts it very simply when he says,

> If the act of justice is to give each man his due, then the act of justice is preceded by the act whereby something becomes his due.

In other words, right comes before justice, and the question we have raised is how we come to have a right to anything. This question is not asked at the superficial and secondary level. At that level one has a right to a house because one has paid the purchase price for it. But the question is how men come to be able to own things like houses at all, that is, to attach things to themselves in a manner which we find nowhere else in nature, things which we cannot detach from them without committing an injustice.

St Thomas drives things right back to the first fundamental truth that, as justice presupposes right, so right presupposes that in the first place man should be there. Before you can have a right you must be. "It is through creation that the created being first comes to have rights." He deduces from this, incidentally, that man had no right to creation and that God owes man nothing, since right and justice are a consequence of creation and do not precede it.

Rights then belong to human beings by virtue of men being there. But we will observe immediately that stones, plants, and animals are also there, yet we do not say that they own things in such a manner as to have a right which justice must preserve. We have therefore to add that men are there in a way which is *sui generis*, and we must try to describe more accurately the mode of thereness of human beings.

Every being is a being in the world. It is an activity related to the other activities about it. And the greater degree of life or activity any being possesses, the more it can be said to "make" the world by which it is surrounded. Life is an activity which makes things surrounding the living being relevant. Many things are relevant to a plant which are not relevant, or much less relevant, to a stone: water, air, light, soil nutrition and so on. One is tempted to say that a plant has a much better idea of what water is than a stone. An animal in turn has a wider world than a plant. It has senses like that of sight, it is not rooted to one spot, it builds lairs and nests. To say that it is more responsive to more things is to say that it has made itself a wider world, or, if you like, that it has a better idea of the world than a plant.

Notice that with this expansion of the animal's world

adumbrations and foreshadowings of the relation of ownership begin to come in. A swallow has a nest, a leopard has a den, squirrels have young in a sense in which a plant does not have seedlings. By a greater penetration into their surroundings they have established a greater relevance of these surroundings to themselves. Whether we say that animals have penetrated the world more deeply than stones or that the world has penetrated them more deeply comes to the same thing. The hold on the outer world corresponds to the level of activity in the inner world. The more self-contained the latter, and the more it is a principle of autonomous organisation, as contrasted with the mere pushes and pulls and chemical interference to which a stone is subject, the more does a living being "possess" its world. The outer world grows with the inner world.

This is a very important principle and suggests that the notion of ownership and consequently of justice is something primordial and analogous. To each his own, and we see now that "own" corresponds to the degree of activity or life which constitutes the "owner".

Let us now turn to man. He is also a being in the world, but it is an ampler world because it is constructed by an ampler life. Man possesses senses like the animal, but his senses have been vastly extended by the use of various technical devices, like microscopes and telescopes and the great range of electronic inventions. Similarly, his organs of response, his hands for instance, have been indefinitely extended by what we can broadly call tools. This extension is possible because man possesses reason as well as sense, and reason is the capacity to get beyond the immediate appearances of things. For instance, he can go backwards in time as archaeologist or historian, or outwards in space by means of using thought and language.

In order for him to do this, the world must be in him in a manner corresponding to the activity of his inner life, and this is an activity of intelligence. To the greater inwardness of life corresponds a greater penetration into, or possession of, the inwardness of things. St Thomas derives the word *intelligere* from *intus legere*, to read within, or read the inside of. To have intelligence is to get hold of the natures of things, which is all that we mean when we metaphorically speak of their insides.

Man can get the universe into himself because he can get himself into the universe. The mind can, as it were, become all things because all things can get into the mind by the action upon them of the intelligence. Man possesses the world more inwardly and more radically than any other terrestrial being because he is capable of the truth about things. Truth is the ultimate foundation of ownership and of justice, and hence we cannot depart from justice without harming man at the very root and core of his being. What he is as spirit or intelligence is destroyed by injustice. A will to justice is nothing less than a will to live, whether individually or nationally or internationally. Further, the right to life is the right to go on possessing the world into which we have entered by intelligence. Justice is not an expedient: to each his own is a metaphysical necessity which man cannot evade because he is man.

Let us revert to a principle mentioned above: "own" corresponds to the degree of activity or life which constitutes the "owner". The more self-contained the inner world, the more does a living being possess his world. What I wish to say is that there is a proportion between a man's "self-possession" and his possession of the world. Every man possesses the world, has a right to the world. For man, knowledge of the nature of things goes linked with self-consciousness. Knowledge implies the conscious unity of the self. Now, self-consciousness is a kind of falling of being within itself, a grasp of being by itself. Intelligence is reflexive: it grasps itself in grasping other things, and it possesses these things by the grasp with which it grasps itself. It is at once and by the same act self-centred and other-centred. It loves others as it loves itself.

Man possesses the world by the same act and by the same right with which he possesses himself. His absolute right to justice, to have what is his own, is posited by the act by which he is. Now we can see more clearly why St Thomas says that justice presupposes creation, for it is by creation that men are there, as intelligent acts of existence. The right to justice and the obligation to do justice are founded in the act by which God is God. By justice men are justified. By justice they possess their own souls and the universe of truth for which they were created. By injustice they are divided from themselves, and plunge into a world of disorder and illusion.

The notion that every man possesses the world, or has a right to the world, is capable of a grave misinterpreta-

8 : ON JUSTICE AND HUMAN RIGHTS

tion. What it becomes, for instance, in the hands of Hobbes or Callicles, is too well known to require statement. Individualist interpretations have been common. They give rise to the ultimate injustice of a tyrant or tyrannical race or nation which seeks to have power over everyone or everything for the purpose of using the world with reference to themselves. This is the notion of autonomy or "self-possession" driven to lunacy. Fully to set out the case against it would require a considerable excursus both into ethics and into epistemology.

In ethics one would have to demonstrate the dependence of the cardinal virtues on humility, which is a habit of placing oneself, with objective realism, in a universe which is *given* and not created by ourselves. It is very revealing to consider what happens to the traditional notion of humility in the system of Hobbes. It becomes a sense of powerlessness to grab the world for oneself. Epistemologically one would have to show that the process of interiorising the world, of making it one's own, is a process by which the mind surrenders itself to the natures of things.

The history of epistemological imperialism is fascinating but long,* and it must suffice to say that the position which the writer occupies is that we do not have a multiplicity of private worlds each having no room for the other,

---

*   One can learn a good deal about it from Roszak's *Where the Wasteland Ends*.

but that the world to which we each have an absolute claim is the same world. It is the same world claiming each of us in different ways. Each makes his own world in a relative and not in an absolute fashion, because the person who makes it is himself given in the world.

Our creation of our world does not extend beyond an active location of ourselves in a common order, a putting of ourselves there where we are. Because he can take the world into himself by intelligence, every man is a world. That is what we mean by calling him a person. But it is the same world seen from the unique angle of every man's existence. That is why every man is my *alter ego*, in the very depth of my own act of being. We live in the same world and we are each other's. What I possess I possess for all, just as what is true for one is true for all; and my absolute right to have justice is inseparable from my absolute duty to do justice.

Every person then is the whole and since the whole includes other persons we can say that men are social by a metaphysical necessity. Society is a whole of wholes, and it is just because every man has an absolute claim to truth and justice, that is, to his proper world, that justice to each is the concern of all. We cannot do injustice to anybody without damaging both ourselves and the structure as a whole of persons.

It is on this absolute inalienability of the right to justice that the doer of injustice must break himself. He does harm to somebody when he commits an injustice but he does incomparably more harm to himself by cutting himself off from his inner relation to other men and to truth. He must close his ports to the universe and to other men, and find his satisfaction in spurious pleasures and ambitions. However physically healthy he may be, he will be spiritually sick and, since the body too is made for truth, even his physical health may be precarious.

This holds for nations as well as for individual men.

This is not a discovery of modern philosophers and psychologists. The relations of medicine and injustice and the connected notion of egoism as a cosmic outrage were fundamentally explored by Plato in the *Gorgias*, from which we can very relevantly quote Socrates, where he says,

> My principle ... runs like this: my dear Callicles, to receive a box on the ears wrongfully is not the greatest of outrages, nor even to fall into the hands of a murderer or a pickpocket; ... to do injustice to another is a far greater evil for the doer of the injustice than it is for the victim.

The question may now well be asked: can one enumerate human rights in their particularity, and can one state what in the concrete we must do in order to do justice? The answer to the latter part of this question is that every man's decisions must be his own. Man is man in a situation, surrounded by all the concrete and material circumstances which make his life the particular life that it is. What is relevant to the decisions as to what is just in respect to any man is the fact that he is John Smith, doing such a job, and circumstanced so-and-so; and that you who must do the act of justice are also a particular man in a particular relation to John Smith. Every moral act is an inalienably personal act whose creativity consists in realising what ought to be done in the given circumstances. If you owe John Smith five pounds, that is a particular historical situation, and what you must do is to pay John Smith five pounds. You cannot do justice in the abstract.

Every act of justice, being a moral act, is in the technical sense of the word, a *prudent* act. Prudence is the first of the cardinal virtues, and is the habit by which we make use of the circumstances at hand in order to realise the good. Morality, of which justice is a part, has always to do with action, and therefore with the concrete and historical.

In the first place it is the *person* who acts and every person is unique in the sense that his make-up differs from that of every other. Secondly, his circumstances and the demands made upon him vary with every man. Every man by virtue of his human nature must seek the good and do justice, but he has to do so by means of an *action*, and action has to use the materials provided by the situation.

Just as an artist has to realise the beautiful through the medium of the particular block of stone or tray of pigments to hand, so the moral man has to shape the situation to hand. Now philosophy can give general rules, and attempt to categorise situations, but the burden of decision always rests on the individual, who has to achieve fidelity to himself and his unique situation. "Thou shalt not steal" is a general rule, but whether a particular situation is a "stealing situation" has to be decided anew each time.

Thus Aquinas writes,
If the necessity is so urgent and evident that instant relief should be afforded, if, for instance, a person is about to collapse and no other way appears of satisfying his want, then he may take, either openly or secretly, what he needs from the possessions of another, nor is this strictly speaking theft or robbery.

We require equity to correct our categorising, and on the analysis given here what is equitable is what will bring men nearer to the truth, or give them an ampler universe in which to live.

Because morality rests primarily on a personal decision, justice begins at home. The great injustices are the cumulative expression of the injustices done in particular personal relationships. It is by the countless threads of right relationships that a sound fabric of society is woven. Rules for just action are in a certain sense a contradiction in terms since rules are general and abstract whereas action is concrete and existential. In a sound society it is the rule which is secondary to the infinite exigencies of human relationships, which, because of the variety of human nature and situation, escape our categorising. Every man has to realise truth in action for himself, and justice is such action as it bears upon other human beings. There is no substitute for a vision which sees oneself in cooperation with others for the realisation of a world of common truth.

Justice, then, is to be thought of personalistically but not atomistically. Justice is owed by one individual to another, but also by the individual to various groups, and by the group to the individual. As well as commutative justice, there is legal or general justice, and distributive justice. If every man owns the world, so do the totality of men, and so do various groups between the individual and the totality. The reason for this is that no one can find the truth by himself. For whatever a man owns he is indebted to men, and their mutual claims must be adjusted.

That no one can find the truth himself but only for himself can perhaps best be developed in the following way. We saw that to have the truth is to get into the natures of things. Now man is a rational *animal*, an embodied being, and to know things he must use his body. It is a commonplace of some schools of philosophy that knowledge begins with sense experience, but this is still too passive a view of knowledge. There is a sentence in St Thomas which will bear further development, and indeed one wishes that he had developed it further himself.

Man, he says, has an intellect and hands. When he says this he intends us to understand that there is a connection between having an intellect and having hands. Just as we cannot get to the natures of things except by the help of the senses, neither can we do so except by manipulating them. The scientist in his laboratory does not simply look at things, he manipulates them, and there is a close connection between the structure of human knowledge and the structure of the human hand. Some have said that man has the kind of knowledge which he has because he has an opposable thumb. At any rate we may notice that to have a knowledge of the natures of things is accompanied by a certain versatility in respect of them. If I leave a knife out in the garden the birds take no notice of it. If I see a child go out, pick up the knife and start cutting with it, I say that the child knows what a knife is.

The variety of things we can handle and the variety of ways in which we can handle them are indications of our superior grasp of the natures of things. A swallow can do something with mud. But man has invented hundreds of muds with which he can do a vast number of things, not to speak of the thousands of other materials which he can use. When we say that he has a concept of mud we mean, among other things, that he can do a great deal with it. The truth about mud is something which he possesses in action. We can say that he possesses mud by using it.

We have established a connection, then, between ownership, use, and the spiritual or personal character of man which we have described as his capacity to go out to things or to know them. Man establishes a claim upon things which must in justice be recognised because he can use them. We say that this nest belongs to this swallow because he has built it. Likewise, man, by putting himself and his intelligence into the materials which the world offers him, comes to own the world. God's claim to the absolute ownership of the universe, so that all things must in justice be referred to him, rests on his not simply using a pre-existing material but creating it *ex nihilo*.

At any rate, we recognise that a thing becomes a man's by his putting himself into it. I am not speaking for the moment about legal ownership, but about something more primitive upon which legal ownership rests. If I pick up a piece of driftwood and carve it into something, that piece of sculpture is mine. A garden that I work myself is more truly mine than one that is worked for me by a gardener. No wonder that hired gardeners are sometimes possessive. When Handel was accused of pirating other people's tunes, he replied, "Well, but the fools didn't know how to use them!"

I may say that a great many difficulties are lurking here. If the tunes were protected by copyright, would that have been an infringement of Handel's rights as a creative composer? Again, if a primitive people is occupying a territory, would a more civilised nation be entitled to aggression on the grounds that it could use the territory more intelligently? Or again, if a man possesses a large estate which is lying idle, could he be dispossessed on the grounds that the estate really belongs to those who can use it? Again, can the workers in a factory say that because they are making the goods they should own them?

One must not jump to any hasty conclusions as to the connection between natural or metaphysical ownership, and legal ownership. It is in fact a very complicated relationship both in history and in theory. It remains true, however, that the final norm of legal justice is natural justice, which rests on the metaphysical capacity to appropriate the world; and the problem of legal justice is to see that every man or group gets that to which his capacity and his intelligent efforts entitle him. There is no sense in one swallow having enough mud for two nests, and another having no mud at all. If there is a connection between truth and handling, then we serve truth by a justice which gets the right hands on the right things, the criterion of right being what enlarges the common universe through enlarging the world of the individual to whom right is done.

When we say, then, that no man reaches truth by himself, we can make a connected statement that no man manipulates things by himself. If a man clears a piece of primitive jungle and plants it, he establishes a claim to it, but he also owes something to the men who made his axe and to the wife who was cooking for him while he did it. If he clears it with the help of a partner, they have a common ownership of the field. The group which effects something may be much larger, with a corresponding larger distribution of ownership, and it may be connected in all sorts of ways with other groups which have a nearer or more distant relevance. This growth and complication adds to our versatility in handling things, that is, to a deeper comprehension of their natures, that is, to a deeper insight into truth.

From this point of view justice in society is truth in action, and the failure legally to recognise natural right will lead to a growth in falsehood, scientific, philosophical, moral and theological. Ultimately, to say that man has both hands and an intellect, is to say that, if you do not get the right hands on the right things, you will not get the right intellects on the right things. For us humans truth is grubbed out of the earth, and those who stand nearest to the earth will in the long run determine culture and effect their salvation. *Exaltavit humiles*. A metaphysician will only get his head into heaven by keeping his feet on the ground.

Plato is a great proponent of this truth in spite of certain very real obstacles in his position. These obstacles are principally the opposition of sense and knowledge, with the consequent playing down of the role of the body in knowledge; and his contempt of what I may call the handling classes. It is the latter which has laid him open to the charge of furthering the growth of tyrannies, and, indeed, if what I have said is true, contempt of the hands will lead to a contempt of justice, and that always leads to tyranny.

But we must remember that Plato's principal aim in politics was to combat tyranny, and that the *Republic* concludes with one of the most devastating onslaughts ever made on the tyrant. What is the basis of this onslaught? It is the clear conviction that men and society are made for truth, and that the end of society is man's insight into the truth.

The *Republic* is a treatise on justice. It is equally and at the same time and for the same motives a treatise on truth. Neither does it entirely neglect the hands. Plato argues that justice begins to make its appearance among men by the division of manual labour and the association of men through the growth of specialised techniques.

The principle of justice in Plato is "to each his own

work", and he tries to relate the work of each to the work of all in the light of a common glory of participation in the truth which each will find in the work and action which express his particular capacity to appropriate the world. For him, too, truth is appropriation of reality. That is the fount of all ownership; and to do justice to a man is to safeguard his share in this appropriation, whether his particular road to truth is through his hands or through his head.

9 : Reflections on Evolutionary Knowledge

Unde alius est actus quo intellectus intelligit lapidem, et alius est actus quo intelligit se intelligere lapidem.

(Hence the act by which the mind knows a stone is one thing, but the act by which it knows that it knows a stone is another. AQUINAS, *SUMMA THEOLOGICA*, 1.87.3)

Any theory of evolution would seem to involve minimally at least these assertions: that there is a present state of affairs, and a past state of affairs, and that the present state of affairs has risen out of the past state of affairs in a manner which can be rationally demonstrated. I think it would be usual to consider the present state of affairs as exhibiting a higher degree of development than the foregoing, though this is not an easy statement to develop.

If we mean merely that the present state of affairs has been preceded by more goings-on than any previous state of affairs, then the statement is merely trite, because that is what we mean by the present state of affairs. If, on the other hand, we mean that the present state of affairs is higher, or more accomplished, or more significant, or better than the foregoing, we are making use of a number of terms which are very difficult to define.

9 : REFLECTIONS ON EVOLUTIONARY KNOWLEDGE

I do not think it is immediately necessary to press the latter point. If we consider our present situation to be privileged, as we do, it must be because it self-evidently claims some value which validates our efforts to establish its antecedents and find out how it came about. We are in effect asking, why and how do I come to be doing what I am at this moment doing? And if this doing did not strike us as valuable, though the value be that of a questioning, we would not inquire further about it. It is because we are constructing something at the moment that we have an interest in reconstructing what led up to this moment, for this reconstruction is a present construction.

This brings me to the notion which I wish to develop, that of reconstruction. Any evolutionary theory involves reconstruction. We have to establish what the state of affairs was, say, 100 000 years ago. Could we say that we are trying to remember how things were then? Of course, we cannot put it this way if we are to mean, by remembering, recalling or re-experiencing what was previously a matter of experience, since among other things we are looking for the antecedents of human experience. However, we are trying to *recall* something, and attempting to extend the range of time suggested to us by our memory of what we have experienced. We are attempting to reconstruct what anteceded experience *as if we had experienced it*. We are saying: that is what it would have looked like had you been there to see it.

There is a question, then, as to how we can extend the range of our experience to what nobody has experienced, and how we can recall what we and indeed the human race cannot remember. In fact, as regards the memory of the human race, we have no right to assume that we remember things in the same manner as, say, an Ancient Egyptian, or, if recalling is an extension of remembering, that we recall things in the same manner. Looking at things the other way round we might suggest that the different way in which an Ancient Egyptian would recall things, for instance, in writing history and in not writing prehistory, could be a clue to the way he remembered. At any rate, our own investigations into prehistory have influenced psycho-analytical theories as well as techniques of remembering.

Let it be clear at once that there is no question of the legitimacy of the effort of recall, because I could not make the statement that there was a period before human experience, without reliance on such recall or reconstruction. Nevertheless problems do arise as soon as we realise that we are extrapolating how we look at things now, in the reconstruction of the appearance of things before they could be experienced. Further, we are trying to transpose ourselves in time, and to make a contemporary way of looking at things operative in some other period.

For instance, we say in imagination: if I could look in at an Aurignacian cave dwelling, this is what I should see. Or: if I were in a carboniferous swamp, this is how things would look. But things would look different to the Aurignacian himself. He would look at and attach a different importance to different things in the environment. In the swamp there would be no human at all. If there was a view of things it would be a Diplodocus-eye view, and what that is like I wouldn't know.

This is, perhaps, put too abruptly, and I shall qualify it considerably later. We must remember how much of modern philosophy is built on the doctrine of the privacy of sensations. In order to construct a public world on the basis of measurement, we made the secondary qualities private and incommunicable. But there is nothing self-evident about it. Indeed, one may wonder how a position so far removed from common sense ever achieved the status of a dogma. By means of it we constructed a world with which we could not communicate directly, and about which we could not speak to each other in ordinary language. But, in fact, if you say to me, this is red, or that is sweet, I know directly what you mean. I have an immediate certainty of the likeness of our sensations, and our common world is principally a world of sensation.

Behind the other view lies a doctrine of exclusive egoisms which is more than suspect. I know what your sensation of red is like because I have one of my own. But to have one of my own is not something which separates me from you but joins me with you, since the dimension of "my own" is common to all human beings. I know directly what it means and so have a direct entry into your world. I know what your sensation of red is like with immediate certainty. It is true that I can raise puzzles about it, but any puzzle which I may raise will assume its truth, and will be stated in language which arose within the sensed world.

One can go further than this. "My own" does not apply only to human beings but to everything. A is A, everything is its own, and has its own world in a sense which I shall elucidate later. Hence I can communicate directly with everything on the basis of "my own". Since I communicate directly with myself by virtue of self-consciousness, self-consciousness is inseparable from direct other-consciousness, and is the principle of the construction not of private worlds but of a public world.

At the root of knowledge lie a cognitive sympathy with and a direct entry into the experiences of not only other human beings but of non-human beings. Hence we try to recall, that is, make ourselves present to, the Diplodocus looking at things. I look out of the window and I see a tree. I try in my mind's eye to see some ancient long-perished fern in the same way. No one in fact ever saw the living fern, and I am trying to supply with my experience the experience which then was absent.

It should be clear that I am not denying that this is possible and profitable. I could not speak of a time before there was human experience if it were not. But we ought to ask what we are doing. We are trying to call all history into the presence of our present way of looking at things. Yet on the evidence of evolutionary investigation there is an evolution of our way of looking at things. There is such a thing as an evolution of consciousness and of self-consciousness. Our very capacity to call other times into our own presence brings before us a sense of how local and how relative is our capacity to do this.

There is no legitimate transition from this statement to an easy and in the long run quite stultifying relativism. It would be absurd to say that there was a Diplodocian viewpoint, and an Aurignacian viewpoint, and a Medieval, and a modern evolutionary, and that there will doubtless be others, and that there is no finality anywhere. There is no finality, but there may be a growth in scope and objectivity which may be precisely in proportion as the thinker can rise to a correct estimate of what and where and when he is, and of what he is doing. To locate our subjectivity in this manner is a prerequisite of objectivity. What I might call the higher relativism is precisely what is necessary to make our knowledge stand firm, and destroy an old-fashioned and naive subjectivism. There comes a point, a very important point in the evolution of consciousness, when thinking about things can progress further only with the aid of thinking about thinking.

Let us try the aid of a diagram (*overleaf*).

By and large, and whatever we may have lost, we can say that the present of modern man is a much richer present than the present of Aurignacian man. Now, the present is for man never a bare present. It is enriched by the retrospects and prospects which go out from and return upon it. The present is full of the past and the future, and our reactions to things here and now depend on our powers of recall and anticipation. The Aurignacian present is relatively poor because it does not contain much past and future. For one thing, my present can call the Aurignacian present into its presence, whereas the con-

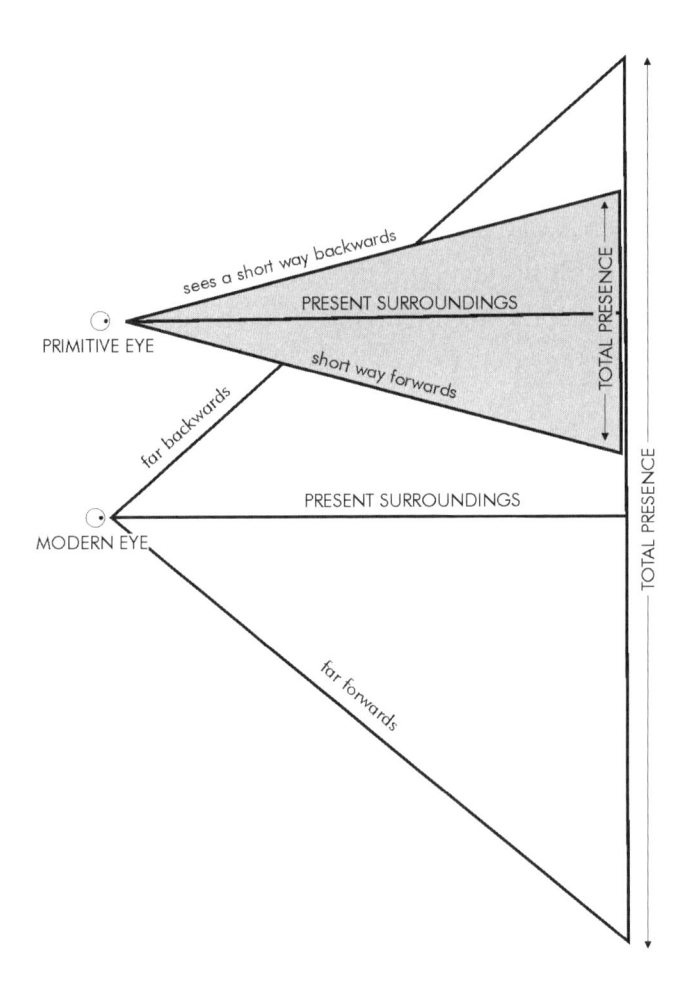

[Figure: Two diagrams comparing a "PRIMITIVE EYE" and a "MODERN EYE". The primitive eye has a narrow cone labeled "sees a short way backwards" and "short way forwards", enclosing "PRESENT SURROUNDINGS" with "TOTAL PRESENCE" marked on the right. The modern eye has a much wider cone labeled "far backwards" and "far forwards", enclosing "PRESENT SURROUNDINGS" with a larger "TOTAL PRESENCE".]

trary is not true. I live him out in a way in which he does not live me out. In short, I contain him in a way in which he does not contain me. That is what we mean when we say that we live later. There is a sense in which the scope of my viewpoint envelops his. In me, his viewpoint is shifted forward in time, and in a sense I am seeing for him.

This notion of the vicarious inclusion of the past in the present seems to me very important. If on the one hand it is true that I impose my presence and my way of looking at things on the past, and perhaps in some degree deform it, I must remember that the past and my own ancestors are also present and working in me, and that their viewpoint is asserting a claim to rise to fuller self-consciousness in me. If there is an imposition, it works from both ends. Their mutual adjustment constitutes objectivity. Living later in time is a privilege which has its responsibilities.

There is a passage in St Augustine's *City of God* which is inexhaustible in its suggestiveness:

> But though the unreasonable creatures' senses contain no knowledge, yet some likeness of knowledge there is in them. But all other corporal creatures, having no sense in themselves, but being the object of others' senses, are therefore called sensible, and the growth and power whereby the trees draw nourishment, this is like their sense. But these and all other corporal bodies' causes are hid in nature; indeed their forms, in which the beauty of the invisible world lies, are apparent to us, *seemingly professing a desire to be known since they could not know themselves*: but our bodily senses judge not of them though they apprehend them. (XI.27)

St Augustine is here pointing to the vicariousness and therefore the responsibility of human knowledge. What accounts for the urge to knowledge is not only the constitution of man to call things into his presence, or to make himself present to things, but also the mute appeal of things to make themselves present to man and to realise their presence to themselves in him, to be taken out of their time into the time of present thought. If we call the past into our presence, the past is also calling us into its presence as its spokesman. That is why in St Augustine self-knowledge and consciousness are inseparable from other knowledge and consciousness, so that Augustinian introspection and knowledge of other things, men and times proceed *pari passu*. There can be no cultivation of self-knowledge without science, and *vice versa*.

In St Augustine's view our present and our presence to ourselves include the "point of view" of all subhuman creation and of all history previous to ourselves. There are elements in Hegel of which he would approve.

I realise that to speak of a stone's point of view may seem strange. But every being has or rather *is* a point of view. That is, it is a focus upon which certain influences converge, which catches them up, so to speak, though the influence may not be sentiently experienced.

We are, in fact, calling attention to a very fundamental metaphysical characteristic of all things, in whatever time they may occur, and we shall have to look at it at some length. This cat is this cat. This stone is this stone. This cat is not this stone. Being themselves is what all beings have in common. A is A and not B. Of course there may be A's which can become B's. But that is a further matter. In any event change would not be real if something did not become something other. The identity of a thing with itself at any moment would appear to be its most obvious as well as its most general characteristic.

Now this would appear to involve that every being of which we have or can have experience is finite. Of every thing it can be said that it is not another thing. A shoe is not a ship, and a cabbage is not a king. A thing in being itself is always not something else. Its nature excludes other natures. In being itself it lacks the nature of something else. And this is what it means to be finite.

The question can be raised whether *to be* necessarily involves to be finite, and whether an infinite being is a contradiction in terms. We shall not follow this question here because we are talking about the things of our experience.

But being finite does not mean having no relation to other finite entities. A king is not a cat, but a king may *possess* a cat, and the cat may *look* at the king. To be finite means not only to exclude but also to stand in need of other things. The world of finite things is a world of relationships and interactions. Our universe is a universe of finite things in a state of constant interaction, sustaining, defining and destroying each other. Things have different degrees of relevance for each other, in the sense for instance that hydrogen and oxygen are relevant to each other.

Being finite means repelling some things as inimical and moving towards some things as amicable. I eat bread but I reject gravel. Hence all struggle, frustration, completion and aspiration derive from finitude. We can say, then, that any finite thing is not merely for itself, but other things are for it, and it for other things. A finite thing can neither exist nor be conceived in isolation from others. These bonds are very various and heterogeneous. Cats and cabbages are differently related to kings.

Furthermore, these relationships fall into groups. Things group themselves or fall into systems by virtue of relevance to each other. Science rests on the existence of areas of mutual relevance which we can isolate for purposes of study. A thing, A, may be closely connected with B and C, but not have the same relevance to O and P. A B C will then form a significant system, but A O P not.

Let us take an example of a system.

> It will be agreed that physical systems exist. We speak, for example, of the solar system, and the term denotes a group of planetary bodies whose movements are so completely interdependent that we can view them as the diversified expression of a single complex process. In order to understand the behaviour of any individual in the group we must consider it in the light of its changing relations to all the others; we must *think* the moving bodies together, and view the sequent phases of their motions from the standpoint of determinant and determined.
>
> The principle involved is as follows. Each planetary orbit ... has an identity of its own, which is determined by, and in turn determines, the identity of every other orbit.*

---

* A.A. Bowman, *A Sacramental Universe*, pp. 36–7. I quote this out of *pietas* to an old teacher and a great man.

Here the planets and the sun are taken as implementing each other through their mutual relevances, and forming a system of finite things.

Our central principle, however, is that to be finite is precisely not to be isolated. Things are marked off from each other in order to be conjoined. Accordingly we must think of a finite thing under three ideas:

1. A finite thing is acted upon by other things; not equally, of course, by all things, as we have just said, but by certain things in certain degrees and ways.
2. It bears in itself the marks or characteristics of other things. It would not be itself unless it pointed to other things, or carried aspects of them in itself. That is, every finite thing is a mirror of others. Thus every man mirrors ideas and so contains in himself his universe. In this way the universe is a society where the being of each is impressed on the being of all. A stone is a *zoon politikon*.
3. Every finite thing acts upon, impresses aspects of itself upon, other things.

1. A FINITE THING IS ACTED UPON BY OTHER THINGS

Take the instance of a stone. Try to conceive of it as not acted on by anything. It would simply disappear. Gravity holds it in place, and makes its parts cohere. Its colour would go if no light fell on it.

Again, a plant requires light, air, water, soil, which act upon it and enable it to unfold its own being.

> Again,
> A geometric figure is clearly determined by the adjoining parts of space, and if the bounds they set to it are removed its essential character is lost. Most natural things can survive a certain amount of such alteration, but there is a very narrow limit to their power. And even when one special limit is partly irrelevant, some other equally external boundary is what constitutes the fact. Gold, for instance, may remain gold in spite of certain alterations of figure, but it is constituted by another limit. Its specific gravity is a term which we use to indicate the comparison between the particular effects which the attraction of the earth exercises on gold and on water. If the action of this outside force were altered so that it produced a different effect on gold, the specific gravity would change and the essence of the metal would be lost ... Everything refers beyond itself endlessly for its explanation.
> (H.A. REYBURN, *Hegel's Ethical Theory*, pp. 76–7)

It may also refer forwards in time.

2. EVERY FINITE THING IS A MIRROR OF OTHERS

It bears the imprint of their natures in itself. Thus a stone mirrors its surroundings in the sense that it would not be itself if its surroundings were different. Thus limestone would disappear in the neighbourhood of certain acids. The stone would not be the size and shape it is had it not been broken and weathered by other bodies. Thus we can tell from the scratches on some pebbles that they were once in a glacier. They have an imprint of the glacier on them. Again, some stones are artefacts, and mirror the life and condition of the primitive men who made them. We can read from them something about the environment in which they were used.

If so to carry traces were not of the essence of every thing, we could never find the cause of any effect, nor perform operations like restoring a fossil skull given a fragment of it.

However, no finite thing is simply a collection of the aspects or effects of other things. It is not merely a vacant locus where certain aspects or perspectives or influences of other things come together. It is not simply a point of view. It has a nature of its own which determines what impress it will take, or how it will mirror what surrounds it. Hence it must be like itself before it can be like other things. How could it act upon other things if it were a mere meeting ground of aspects of these things? Every being has a proper structure which is a principle of selection of its own experiences. The fact that a blow is mirrored by a stone as a mere mechanical push, and is internalised by me as an impression of pain, is in each case a mirroring differing with respect to the nature of the subject.

If things are merely collections of aspects of other things, foci in which certain perspectives come together, then we have to answer the questions: how perspectives came to collect at these foci; and why just *these* perspectives came to collect there, that is, why the perspective should present itself at this focus and with just this configuration. If we call the presence of a perspective at a particular focus a perception, to what does that perception refer or what does it intend if everything is at first nothing but a vacant focus? Whence came the first aspect that is taken up in a perception?

If things are *merely* bundles of perspectives of other things, then we must posit an inexplicable precipitation *ex nihilo* of at any rate one perspective, and of absolutely abstract formless, contentless foci at which the perspective will appear in various guises, where there is nothing in the receiving point to account for the differentiation. Or we must attribute to the perspective power to appear at various "places" in a fashion which will characterise that place.

It is necessary, therefore, to attribute a primary act of existence to every focus which is at the same time an original point of view with an active power of selecting relevant perspectives. The idea of a finite thing involves the idea of a multiplicity of such foci of existence, or immanently characterised "places", since a finite thing cannot be conceived in and through itself. The proper being of things is thus a principle of the selection of "perceptions", and constitutes a *modus percipiendi*. They undergo change in time by the assimilation of perceptions.

Some philosophers, raising the question whence each thing derives its proper force or activity of existence, by which its various relevancies are determined, refuse to entertain any conception of spontaneous generation or original ultimate and brute presence, on the grounds that this is irrational. They hold that one must posit an original being by imaging whose existence each finite being is itself, and consequently the fellow of every other, as members of one society.

Such a being would have to depend on nothing but itself for its perceptions, which would therefore be perceptions of itself, and which would thus be completely self-conscious intelligence whose existence was its own object or word. The advantage of this position is that it removes the grounds for the absurd controversy of creation versus evolution by laying the foundation of a conception of evolution as concreation by analogous percipience.

3. THINGS ACT UPON OR ALTER OTHERS

Cows eat grass, sodium acts on water. Or take our stone again: it may obstruct the flow of water in a gully, prevent a plant from coming up, and so on. In the sense in which we are using the term, the deflected water, as deflected, images or takes the imprint of the stone. This could not happen were agent and patient not in some way "like" each other. Thus the stone and the water have materiality in common.

St Augustine would say that they must in a sense love each other. That is why he says that weight is to a body as love is to a soul. Again, the mind which mirrors things in knowing has a liking for being and truth.

The environment of any finite thing is the other things with which it is in interaction. Thus the wounded traveller in the scriptural story was more truly part of the Samaritan's environment than of the Levite's. The Samaritan reacted more deeply, thereby making the traveller his neighbour.

We may say, then, that every finite thing is acted on by or suffers its environment; reflects or mirrors it from its own point of view; and reacts upon it, that is, impresses its structure as a perspective upon other things. Thus every finite thing has three fundamental attitudes to its world. These attitudes are not separable but are all exemplified at any moment of a thing's history. It could not suffer unless it was, nor react upon unless it suffered. Thus a stone affects other things because it has a certain size, weight, and shape, which it has by virtue of its delimitation by other things.

Every finite thing has these three characteristics. They take different forms at different levels of reality. Thus at the level of organic existence the interaction of organism and environment is more immediately noticeable than in the sphere of inorganic existence. The organism can live only at a certain temperature, absorbing certain substances and excreting others. It is always taking out of and putting into the environment according to its special structure, and loses its own character when a too violent transplantation occurs. Biology investigates these three characteristics as they appear in animate things.

Physics investigates them as they appear in animate things.

> A body, says Newton, will remain at rest or retain its constant velocity except as it is influenced by some external force. When it is so influenced, its rate of change of momentum will be proportional to the force impressed. For action and reaction are always equal. In these three principles Newton inaugurated a revolution in the concept of scientific explanation by requiring that any particular natural occurrence should be explained wholly in terms of particular natural circumstances external to it and affecting it.
> (H. MILLER, *Science and History*, P. 56)

What you do is to relate the body to its environment. The force of gravity follows from its likeness to and liking for other bodies. It is behaving as a "social" being.

When it comes to man this still holds true. He forms one society with his universe, reflecting it on the physical and biological levels, but also on the intellectual, mirroring it and its history in ideas and putting back into existence the structures which he has discovered as supporting the appearance and structure of his own thought.

Let us ask how far all this has brought us in solving our original problem. Our problem was that in evolutionary theory we are trying to mirror or represent or recall a past state of affairs when there were no human perceivers, or at any rate, and at a certain stage, perceivers with a different apperceptive mass who lived in an inner and an outer world different from our own. We effect this interpretation in terms of our way of seeing things, that is, we are describing things as seen which were not seen at all, and we are asking how this kind of projection of the present upon the past can claim to be true.

In the words of Owen Barfield:

> We have chosen to form a picture, based very largely on modern physical science, of a phenomenal earth existing for millions of years before the appearance of consciousness. The phenomena attributed to these millions of years are therefore, in fact, abstract models or 'idols of the study'. We may compromise by calling them 'possible phenomena', implying thereby that that was how the world would have looked, sounded, smelt and felt, *if* there had been someone like ourselves present.
>
> (SAVING THE APPEARANCES, P. 135)

We picture to ourselves a world of erupting volcanoes, or miasmic swamps, or ponderous dinosaurs; and yet these are in a sense our volcanoes, and jungles, and animals.

The problem arises from the fact that in a sense there is no such thing as an unheard sound or an unseen colour. Sound and colour arise within the society of men and things. Red is the appearance of something *to* a person, and the experience of red refers to a situation in which there is a person. You cannot have red without a percipient any more than you can have weight without a gravitational pull. How then can we say that 10 000 000 years ago there were brown volcanoes spouting red flames? A volcano is something loaded with anthropomorphic constructions. Owen Barfield would call it a "collective representation". What remains of it if we try to remove it from our society, and in what sense did it exist?*

I may say that I do not doubt that there were volcanoes. I am only trying to find out what the statement means, and how I effect that retrojection of myself in time which represents them as having existed. How do I re-present what was never until now presented?

The answer I should give is along these lines. Granted that there is some validity in the idea that a stone or a plant has or is a point of view, then we cannot say that a volcano was never presented. It was presented to the surrounding landscape. Similarly a prehistoric fern was presented to a pterodactyl. Each *made something of* what was presented to it. This enables us to visualise evolution as a process in which things made something of other things. If we now recall the Augustinian notion of vicarious knowing, and of the gathering up in our own present of the presents or points of view of subhuman beings, then we can say that we were present vicariously at, say, the eruption of the volcano, and are raising the landscape's point of view to a higher degree of actuality (Cf. G.M. Hopkins, 'Ribbesdale'). I am seeing for the landscape. The volcano has been seen. It is my privilege to say what was seen.

If, as I argued earlier, to be is to be in relation to other

---

*   See the conception of Eigenwelt, in *Existence*, ed. May, Angel & Ellenberger, p. 63.

things, then the universe is a totality of reciprocating perceptions, meaning by perception what any being notes or registers of the presence of another being. Thus a hole in a piece of wood is what the wood perceives of the awl. When I see the hole, I can read off "for" the wood what happened to it, but the wood mutely preserves the evidence. It is I who give words to it. The colours and sounds of the volcano do not go unregistered. They are gathered up and passed on in the modifications which they produced in their "percipients", and in this way they have descended to me as their heir. If there is any truth in the theory of evolution then the volcano still reverberates in me, and I am not merely *imposing* my present upon the past, but exposing the past which is present to me, and I am making explicit the links which are "professing a desire to be known".

Lest this outline of a solution should seem wildly speculative, let me take a mundane example to indicate what my main point is. I say that there is a dog lying on the carpet in my study. I will not pursue the interesting vistas opened up by the time-schemes in the statement: there is a pterodactyl perching on the arm of the chair.* We will stick to the dog on the carpet.

Now, this is a thoroughly anthropomorphic statement. I am saying that a dog as a dog is to me, is lying on a carpet as a carpet is to me. There is a sense in which I cannot get

---

* Far too little attention is paid to time factors in epistemology.

inside the dog. We all know the difficulties that arise when we try to give a purely "objective" description of a dog's subjective processes or of a dog's world. We can note, measure, and interrelate reactions, but in a sense we remove ourselves further and further from the subjective dog in this kind of investigation.

In any event, and even in this kind of investigation, I can only get at the dog by virtue of the dog in me. I bear his *vestigia*, and that in two ways. In the first place I also have a bodily and sensory make-up, so that in seeing and smelling him I am bringing my own caninity to bear on him. Secondly, I have an idea of the dog. He is in me in the form of an interpreted perception. He is in me in a way in which he is not in himself, since he lacks this degree of interpretative power. I can say, that is a dog, but the dog cannot say, I am a dog. Any "objective" investigation of the dog rests on the certainty that I know what a dog is. Otherwise I might investigate the cat instead.

The dog from my point of view is more of a dog than he is from his own. I am raising him in existence. Similarly, what is the carpet to a dog? Something soft to lie on. I can appreciate this because of my own caninity, and that is my only approach to what "soft" and "lie on" mean to a dog, though of course I can describe it externally in terms of curling up and so on. But "carpet" does not mean to a dog something bought in 1960, costing so much, made in so and so, and having a design in such and such a tradition. The latter carpet is my carpet, not the dog's carpet, just as the Aurignacian man's cave is my cave and not his cave. I am placing "my" dog on "my" carpet, and whatever I may say about the dog's subjectivity and the dog's carpet must set out from there. I can speak about the dog and his environment only because I have taken them up into my own.

If I can speak about the evolution of myself and my world from other beings and their worlds, it can only be by means of an involvement of myself which gives the past an existence in a manner which is presupposed by any account which I may give of the rise of my existence from that past. If there has been in some quarters a blind and instinctive resistance to the theory of evolution in its nineteenth-century form, it may well arise, to some degree at any rate, from the awareness that, if man is the product of evolution, there is also a sense in which evolution is the product of man, and that he, by his mode of intelligent existence, has raised to existence and intelligibility the very factors in the name of which his own existence, as something *sui generis*, has been denied.

What comes first, at any rate epistemologically, is the present human world, which gives their voice to dogs and Aurignacians and pterodactyls. They cannot be made to speak inhuman words, and that is the solution to Owen Barfield's difficulty that they have been made to speak in human words. What we have to do to found the theory philosophically is to relate it to a self-conscious awareness of where we stand at the moment.

Perhaps I can make the epistemological issue clearer by the help of the theory of knowledge of St Thomas

Aquinas. I think this could be done equally successfully with the aid of modern phenomenological and existentialist epistemologies, but that of St Thomas will serve my purposes; also, the terminology is neater. There is a celebrated Thomist thesis which will bear almost endless expansion. It is: *cognitum est in cognoscente per modum cognoscentis*, the thing known is in the knower according to the way of being of the knower; or, to translate it into the terms I have been using, the way we see things is relative to the point of view, or situation, of the percipient. The Thomist thesis, in fact, does justice to the anthropomorphic character of our knowledge and to the constructive contribution which the human mind makes to existence. It enables us to see our knowledge as human and interpretive while establishing its fidelity to the nature of things. Let us go into this more fully.

The problem of knowledge commences when we start to think about our own thinking; when we commence to put questions like: what do I mean when I say, this is a pencil, or, this rose is red? Any satisfactory answer has to do justice to two essential insights. The first is that I am really saying something about an actual rose or pencil which has an independent existence, that is, that my knowledge is objectively founded and grasps things as they are. The second is that knowing is a creative activity of man, and that in knowing things he is doing something to them. It is very difficult to preserve both insights because at first sight they cannot be reconciled. We know that in apprehending a thing we are subjecting it to certain subjective processes, and yet we all have the natural and immediate conviction that, for example, this pencil really exists as I perceive it to be.

St Thomas wishes to preserve the essential difference between known and knower, without reducing the status of the one to that of the other and yet finding something which is common to both.

He calls our attention to something so commonplace that we seldom pause to meditate upon its importance, namely that this pencil is in me in a manner in which I am not in this pencil. Throughout the whole of nature we find things assimilating other things. Thus men eat peaches, and peaches take in CO_2.

Knowing is a special case of such assimilation. I don't take peaches into my body only but also into my mind. Suppose I go out of the room leaving my pencil on the table. Nevertheless I take the pencil with me – in my head. It has an existence in me distinct from its physical existence on the table. My knowledge of the pencil is a form of existence of the pencil. It also realises a potentiality of my own human existence. It is the characteristic of an intelligence that it can become all things.

For St Thomas knowability is a potentiality of everything which is. To be known is an actualisation of its own nature. To know things, further, is a potentiality of a particular kind of nature, namely, an intelligence. In the process of knowing, both I who know and that which is known are actualised in the line of their own natures. The pencil operates in me in a manner determined by its own nature.

Hence it is the pencil that I know and not my idea of the pencil. Nevertheless it is a potentiality of myself as a knower which is at the same time being actualised. I assimilate the object of knowledge according to the mode of my own being. I therefore know the pencil as it is, but not as an intellectual nature of another kind would know it. Thus St Thomas gives full weight to the subjective factor without prejudicing the directness and the objectivity of our knowing.

Now, what is the mode of my own being? Man is a unity of body and mind, capable of intellectual operations, but compelled by his bodily nature to attain to knowledge only through sense experience. The senses give us particular images of particular things. For instance, I form the image of *this* pencil. But the general conception, or universal "pencil", because it is universal cannot be grasped by sense. There is a difference in kind between images and universals.

St Thomas holds that abstraction of the universal from the image is the work of the *active intellect*. Human knowledge is knowledge of the nature or "quiddity" of things not in itself, as the Platonist and extreme realists hold, but as existing in a particular corporeal matter, that is, to recognise the universal in the sensible. Now, since the nature of a thing is what makes it to be the *kind* of thing which it is, we can say that abstraction consists in the intellect considering in any material thing what constitutes it in its possible species, leaving aside the material principle of individuation which makes it *this* particular thing.

This species or "form" is in a sense, then, an ideal being, but it is nevertheless not a fiction of the mind, but an ideal mode of existence of the sensible thing itself which realises the potentiality of this kind of existence only in a mind. It is not itself an object of thought. It is that *by* which we think: that by which I recognise this object to be *a* pencil. If the mind whose proper nature is to be intelligent can actualise this capacity only through contact with the sensible world, so the object can become intelligible only when its nature is disengaged by a mind.

We can see the resemblance to St Augustine in the notion that the presence of the human mind is necessary to actualise the potentiality of truth in the thing known. Further, if *ens et verum convertuntur*, this must be a placing of the thing known in existence. It is achieving a higher actualisation in our presence. But since it is the *cognitum* which is being actualised, the fact that our knowledge is human knowledge constitutes no bar to its fidelity to the nature of things. But it does justice to the fact that the nature of things includes human presence.

Leaves are green because they form part of a society including men, but it is nevertheless true that it is the leaf which is green, because to show forth greenness is a potentiality *of the leaf* which is exercised only in that society. It is true that the evolutionary dimension of this society is not dealt with by St Thomas, that is, what we should now call the historical character of our knowledge. Obviously, I should not wish to minimise the importance of this, but let us first suck what honey we can out of St Thomas.

It is a well-known and valuable contribution of modern existentialism to show that knowing is a positing in existence of the thing known. But this way of regarding knowledge is already in St Thomas, with at least as great a precision. In order to understand him, however, we have to get rid of certain popular misrepresentations. These are in substance as follows. God alone can create, and he creates in accordance with the divine ideas. His knowledge creates what he knows. Man can know only what God has created, and his function as knower is simply to reproduce what God has put there. We then get an interpretation of the *adequatio* formula in terms of a naive correspondence or copy theory which is in fact not thirteenth century at all, but corresponds rather to the dead and ready-made universe of the deists from which immanent creative movement has been excluded.

Now, St Thomas's epistemology is in a very strict and profound way the epistemology of a created universe, and to understand it we must understand his doctrine of creation and not confuse it with deist theories. We have to remember that for St Thomas secondary causes have real efficacy. God creates a world which resembles him as an effect resembles its cause. Now this cause is a creative cause, and the effects resemble it in having an existence and creativity of their own.

The activity of secondary causes is therefore in a very genuine way concreation, or secondary creation, so that the notion of the universe as possessing immanent secondary creativity is a cornerstone of St Thomas's view of the world. On his view of causality, causality is a bringing into being of new things by other things. That is, every act posits things in existence. Knowing is an act, and knowing posits things in existence in accordance with the nature of the agent, who therefore gives them intelligible existence proportioned to the character of the cause.*

It is true that this cause is a secondary cause. The mind of God, as St Thomas points out in the *De Veritate*, is the measure of things, whereas things are the measure of the human mind. Nevertheless, the human mind genuinely does do something for and to them. In creating things the mind of God gives them a proper and efficacious existence. This is true also of the human mind. Since it is a creature of the divine intelligence, and therefore like it, it shares in the power of calling things into being.

While it cannot absolutely initiate being, it can call

---

* The relation of self-knowledge to knowledge of the external world is profoundly discussed by Aquinas in *Summa Theologica*, 1.87. For St Thomas self-knowledge is an act of positing oneself in existence precisely as a received being. Knowing raises the *cognitum* from potency to act. In self-knowledge the *intellectus* is an *intellectum*. *Intellectus in actu est intellectum in actu propter similitudinem rei intellectae*. But what is a compound of potency and act is received being. Therefore self-knowledge is an act by which a *cognoscens* concreates his own being, an act which at the same time establishes both its likeness to and difference from God. It cannot do this, however, without a prior knowledge of the physical world (V. 1. 87. 3 resp.).

St Thomas thus offers a *via media* between Sartre's "man created himself", and the view that he is the mere product of external causes. Man can neither create his own essence nor reduce himself to the *en-soi*.

things into being in a secondary way. Just as the divine creation is an evocation or speaking of things by the divine mind, so human creation is an invocation of things which brings out or posits their proper activity in a dimension of existence which would not be there were it not for the compresence of the human intelligence, a dimension which would collapse were the human mind removed, just as the whole universe would collapse were it not for the compresence of the divine Logos which speaks it.

In a real sense, then, I give existence to this pencil, and any exposition of the *adequatio* formula which ignores this is, shall we say, inadequate. A God's-eye view of the pencil is both the act which sustains it in being and the mind which knows entirely what it is and what its function is in the totality of creation. A man's-eye view of the pencil is true to its nature, but since its nature is to be efficacious it registers its intelligible efficacity, or its intelligible existence, in a human universe where its relevance to human intentions and human providence is seized as a dimension of what it is.

As an artefact or as a utility in the framework of human intentions and providence it has an intelligibility as existentially disposable which is analogous to the complete disposability of the universe by the divine providence which corresponds to its absolute calling into existence by God. Thus the disposability of things by handling is for St Thomas an indispensable part of the act by which we invoke them into being. The hand as well as the mind is an agent of existence, because it is the whole man that knows. Man as a whole, body and mind, reconstitutes the causal series, both in the theoretical and practical orders. Hence the observation *habet homo intellectum et manum*, man has reason and hands.

The extension of this for our purposes is obvious. If we think also with our hands, and if our hands are evolved in time, then the times speak immanently in our hands, when we use them, for instance, in those investigations which enable us to call the past into the dimension of human being. We are lending them a voice, which expresses their desire to be mirrored in intelligence.

In a previous analysis we pointed out that every finite thing mirrored its environment. In this sense, and by stretching our terms, we can say that every finite thing "perceives" its environment. Further, in its presence the environment is something more than it would be without it. It is more fully actualised.

Let us, again by stretching terms, call every thing in its function as creative mirror, a *cognoscens*. A stone, even, would then be not only a *cognitum* but a *cognoscens*, and there would be an analogy and anticipation of human knowledge in the presence of one stone to another. This would hold also for the presence of a pterodactyl to a stone or to another pterodactyl.

The stone would be present *per modum cognoscentis*, and would at that level, and in an analogous way, be truly known. St Thomas recognises an analogy of knowledge in subhuman beings. But what is perhaps most suggestive is what, looking above man, he has to say about angelic knowledge.

St Thomas maintains that there are beings having a superior mode of knowledge to the human. Here, too, the knowledge must be *per modum cognoscentis*. Now, suppose that an angel perceives this pencil. Not having a human sensory make-up, the angel would "perceive" the pencil differently from the way we do, just as, analogously, we see it differently from the way a dog does. There is an angelomorphic as well as an anthropomorphic and cynomorphic view of the pencil. The pencil is being realised according to the nature of the society in which it is. There can be several sciences of the pencil, each of which will be true, because in each case it will be the pencil which speaks or proclaims its existence, in a manner which accords with the ear of the hearer.*

---

* On the question of the pencil's knowledge of pencils, compare Merleau-Ponty, *Phénoménologie de la Perception*, pp. 82–3:

"Ainsi chaque objet est le miroir de tous les autres. Quand je regarde la lampe posée sur ma table, je lui attribue non seulement les qualités visibles de ma place, mais encore celles que la cheminée, que les murs, que la table euvent 'voir', le dos de ma lampe n'est rien d'autre que la face qu'elle 'montre' à la cheminée. Je peux donc voir un objet en tant que les objets forment un système ou un monde et que chacun d'eux dispose des autres autour de lui comme spectateurs de ses aspects cachés et garantie de leur permanence. Toute vision d'un objet par moi se réitère instantanément entre tous les objets du monde qui sont saisis comme coexistants parce que chacun d'eux est tout ce que les autres 'voient' de lui."

The fact that the sciences are different offers no impediment to saying that each is true, though this would hold only if they were arranged in degrees of lower and higher actualisation, so that the higher actualisation expressed vicariously what was only potential in the lower. That is, the lower *cognoscens* would have to be present to the higher.

We may add, by the way, that the conception of the possibility of several sciences of the same *cognitum* is a way in which St Thomas expresses the objective inexhaustibility of any creature, precisely as creature, that is, as produced from the divine wisdom.* This is the source of its givenness and objectivity. It surpasses the capacity of any *cognoscens* except God, whose Logos therefore is the highest science which calls everything into its presence, and makes final sense of the world. Although this adds a very important dimension to our discussion by calling in the Logos as the final validation of evolutionary theory, I shall not pursue it here.

Let us try another diagram to see where we have arrived.

We have, then, a variety of "perceptions" of the object, varying according to the *modus percipiendi*. But we must call attention to a dimension of this diagram that is more vivid to us than it was to St Thomas, and brings in the

---

* I suspect this is the origin of the Kantian *Ding-an-sich*.

9 : REFLECTIONS ON EVOLUTIONARY KNOWLEDGE

```
DIRECTION OF TIME ↓

A. Stone ─────────────╲
                       ╲  'Perceives'
B. Tree ───────────────╲────────
                        ╲
C. Pterodactyl ─────────────────● OBJECT
                        ╱
D. Aurignacian man ────╱
                       ╱
E. Medieval ──────────╱
                      ╱
F. Modern ───────────╱
```

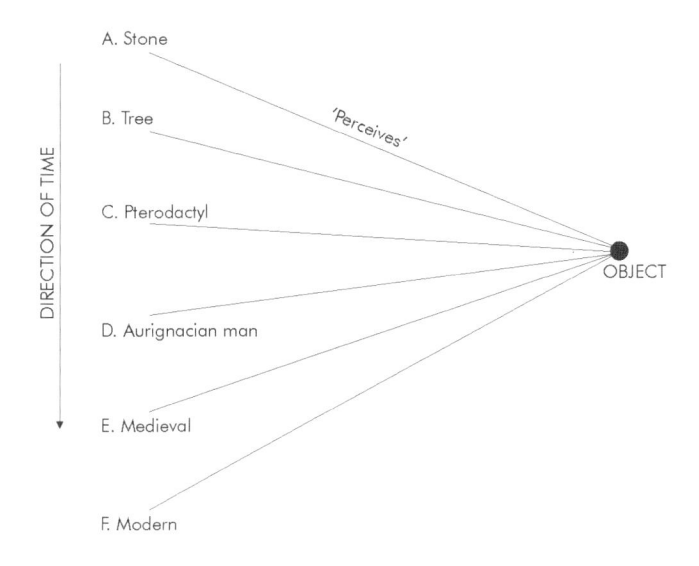

REFLECTIONS ON EVOLUTIONARY KNOWLEDGE

historical dimension to which we adverted earlier. We cannot take this diagram statically. We must also remember that as far as the *cognitum* is concerned there are things for us to see which weren't there for, say, the pterodactyl to see. Thus I have not represented the latter as seeing a pencil. Again, stones were there for pterodactyls to perceive, but there was a time when there were no pterodactyls for stones to perceive. That is, there was an evolution in time of *cognita*. Further, to natural *cognita*, themselves evolving, there were added artefacts. This seems to me very important, and a fuller treatment would require considerable attention to it.

For the moment I wish to call attention to the fact that

the passage from stone to man involves a passage *in time*. Further, as I have just pointed out, this passage in time adds to the number and to the kinds of *cognita*. Thus an Aurignacian man is a *cognitum* for a modern man, though the latter could not be a *cognitum* for an Aurignacian man. The percipients themselves become *cognita*. Further, modern man, to the degree that there is an evolution of self-consciousness, and one of which he is aware, is a *cognitum* for himself. As self-conscious he is a *cognoscens* related to himself as *cognitum*.

In terms of our diagram there is a temporal movement from A to F, and A to F can each and all be taken as O. Further still, *all* the *cognita* of modern man can be regarded as *cognoscentes* insofar as he can recognise in them the analogies and prototypes of his own percipience. *Nihil perceptibile nisi percipiens*. He sees not only stones, but pencils and cave dwellings and his whole ancestry related to himself as *cognoscens*. There is a transformation of the *cognitum* as man advances in self-consciousness and retroactively calls out new dimensions from and gives a new existence to the past. Times change, and the consequence of it is that we can change time. We change it into spirit. If the human spirit can become all things, it can only be by recreating them in its own image. Perhaps this is what Owen Barfield means by final participation.

It is important to notice that, when I say this, I do not mean that the 'O's in the diagram are vaporised into spirit or ideas. I am *not* an idealist. They remain as concrete as ever. I am giving them a more genuine pastness than ever.

Man has a certain relative power of calling things into genuine independent existence. Further, the things of the past persevere in time, not in their proper existence but in their vicars. Thus 'F's include 'A's which have either been incorporated in the 'F's or persist as modified 'A's in the environment of both. For instance, my body includes an element of stoniness and there are stones around me. Things existing at time A have undergone modification, have dropped away in a greater or lesser degree, or been taken up in later modifications.

I cannot accept a transformation of matter into spirit which would destroy its materiality. Thus pterodactyls have dropped away, but there are birds, and there is something reptilian in me. I go upon the earth, if not on my belly. The predecessors of dogs have disappeared, but there are dogs. And so there is a sense in which there can be an actual cynomorphic carpetology, and not a cynodontomorphic carpetology. The construction of an epistemology of the latter would be too speculative for my tastes. A cynodont on a carpet would be a purely spiritual construction and therefore crazy if affirmed in existence. The craziness would consist in a confusion of the times.

True spirituality is true sanity and consists in fidelity to the times. In the re-presentation of the past we have to avoid writing fairy tales. Yet we do try to reconstruct the cynodont's carpetless world. But we do this and have to do this by a retrojection of human percipience. We have to see for the pterodactyl, and derive rules for his epistemology from our own. We may have to do this negatively, but our own knowing remains the standard even when we say that the other's point of view is *not* our own. There is a sort of *via negativa* to be followed in our investigation of subhuman as well as of superhuman nature.

I may add that the speculative construction of a cynodontomorphic epistemology on this principle, while out of this world, might be found to have a relevance to this world comparable with that of Riemannian geometry. At any rate I am sure that St Thomas's speculative construction of an angelic epistemology has vast possibilities for modern theory of knowledge which nobody seems to have had the imagination to grasp. It opens the way to a relativity theory for modern anthropology. The controversies on evolution in the nineteenth century were sometimes represented as the battle of the apes and the angels. The angels came off badly because nobody knew enough about their point of view. A theory of analogous perceptions could solve the controversy to the advantage of both parties.

Medieval man, then, as much as Aurignacian man and the man of the carboniferous swamp, *becomes* the *cognitum* of modern man, who grows in self-consciousness as he finds his own ancestry. They, too, will be known to modern man *per modum cognoscentis*. This *cognoscens* is historically situated, and he knows it. He can perceive and reconstruct the past only from where at present he stands. But I have tried to indicate that he is not on that account merely deforming the past or projecting his own idols upon it, and that for the reason that he is carrying this past in himself and perceiving vicariously for it. He carries it in his own body and mind.

If you like, my carpet and the dog's carpet are both *the* carpet, only mine is more so. That there may be superior carpets, angelic carpets or divine carpets does not invalidate my carpetology. I can relativise it only from the starting point of its own validity. In other words, my science, including my evolutionary science, can be objective and true provided that I situate myself by a true self-consciousness, provided that I recognise my own spirituality, and provided that I recognise the principle of vicarious percipience as a central theme in the evolutionary process. It is by relativising our knowledge to ourselves and recognising it as human knowledge, if you like, created knowledge, and fixing it in time that we establish its objectivity. It has, however, to be established by an act of self-consciousness which requires great effort.

In tackling these epistemological questions which arise out of evolutionary theory we have, I think, thrown some light upon the process itself. Man himself is involved in it, so that the examination of his knowing-processes puts us in firmer possession of data which have themselves to be accounted for. We cannot look at the process with a detached eye, but must see it with an involved eye, and are concerned with the conditions of this involvement. That is, we cannot look at the process without self-consciousness, which involves consciousness of our situation. If we have to look for an explanation of ourselves in terms of the process, it is still more true that we have to look for an explanation of the process in terms of ourselves, and something of what this means I have tried to bring out in this chapter.

In tracing his descent, man is ascending and carrying the process of his descent with him, a process which he *has* to see from the point of view which he has reached here and now. On this account the picture which he forms must be anthropomorphic, *per modum cognoscentis hic et nunc*, since the *morphos* of man is both the subject and object of investigation. I hope that we have heard the end of the quarrel of anthropomorphism versus objectivity. Objectivity is itself a human attitude and a quality of human knowledge. It is itself anthropomorphic and rests on the capacity of an F to relate to itself as an O. It requires a certain self-estrangement, a putting of oneself out of the picture, which fails to be destructive only when we realise from what position in the picture we are carrying out the feat. Hence I have tried to validate and correct the theory from out of the centre of the theory itself. Seeing nature as it is can only mean seeing it as we see it. So much I will concede to Kant.

Where I would differ from Kant is in shifting from a timeless epistemological subject to an historical subject, to an F who has accumulated A B C D E in himself and whose self-knowledge is itself involved in time. This way of looking at things enables us to advance not only on Kant but also on Darwin. Darwin falls a victim to the estrangement of rational man from himself, by his theory of chance variations. Now, nothing could be more unscientific than an appeal to chance because, where chance starts, reason and rational explanation come to an end. When I say that a thing happens by chance I am professing agnosticism with respect to the reasons for its occurrence. We are then condemned to give by means of reason an irrationalist account of the appearance of reason.

But if I regard evolution as the accumulation of "perceptions", which can lead to the appearance of an F who, because he is an O to himself, can give an account of the process, then I am insisting upon the intrinsic rationality of the process. Only men can be irrational, and what irrationality is in essence is a departure from what we are, which cannot be separated from where and when we are. I cannot solve the epistemological problems involved in the human construction of the past unless I can see my theoretical construction of the past as corresponding to a fact, namely the sublation of past worlds into my own world. A theory which destroys itself, as the Darwinian theory does, because it does not square with the fact of the theory itself, that is, because it is lacking in self-consciousness, cannot be properly scientific.

If our theory is to be true then in theory as well as in fact – and because a theory must be true to fact, and in this case, a fact in which it is involved – then it must sublate past worlds into our own world, which is a world that includes evolutionary theory itself. We are trying to represent representations from the point of view of a privileged *cognoscens* whose evolutionary history is a history of "perceptions" or "presences". Evolution then becomes the story of the accumulation of earlier points of view in later, and, when this accumulation finds expression in theory, that theory must, in the words of St Augustine, be adequate to the desire of the facts to be known, a knowing which would be quite impossible if the facts were subject to the irrational factor of chance.

Our whole construction then rests on the act by which F becomes an O to himself. It rests on an act of self-consciousness. The modern man, the *cognoscens*, relates himself to himself as *cognitum*, and if the *cognoscens* forgets that the *cognitum* is a *cognoscens in via* he falls into self-alienation and gives an irrational account of himself. Furthermore, this *cognitum* will be known *per modum cognoscentis*, that is, our knowledge of ourselves will be a *human* knowledge, not a canine or an angelic or a divine knowledge. It is a knowledge by a being of a being which is objectively relative and in time, a knowledge therefore which to be absolute in the sense of true to facts must be relativised.

Knowledge of man by man must in the nature of the case be a knowledge adequate to human modes of knowing, but inadequate to his nature. His *modus cognoscendi* cannot be fully known by him, and he must remain a mystery to himself not because he has not yet acquired enough human knowledge, but because his human knowledge is inadequate to itself. This does not make it untrue, because the human *cognitum* is, by being known, being actualised in the line of its own being. It is the pencil which is red, although it is red only to man, and what man says about himself can be true provided it takes into consideration the *modus recipientis*, under which the *cognitum* is received.

I am arguing, then, that evolutionary theory must introduce the observer in a manner analogous to procedures in modern physics. Epistemological considerations will have to become part of its substance, and what it states will have to be stated in a way which makes explicit the viewpoint from which it is stated. It must become self-conscious by taking the present state of the evolution of consciousness into consideration.

I am aware that I have said very little about the theological issues raised by evolutionary theory, but it should be abundantly clear from my argument that the product of creation cannot, except in a dependent way, be the lord of creation. A theory of evolution which destroyed all divinity would destroy human rationality and therefore destroy itself. This is a very large issue to which I cannot do justice in a conclusion. But if the theory requires a *prise de conscience*, and if that act relativises human knowledge, then that knowledge must be informed by reverence, a reverence which it cannot have for itself compatibly with a genuine realisation of what it is. How far we can have genuine self-knowledge without subordinating the self to God is another of the questions in which St Augustine is a master. If I know myself I know that there is a sense in which I am not, and all my theories are infected with my nothingness.

If I can form a conception of a hierarchy of sciences of

a pencil graded *secundum modum cognoscentis*, I can form a similar conception of a hierarchy of sciences of man. And if I can form a conception of a higher science of pencilology than is possible to man, so I can form the conception of a superhuman anthropology. Just as a pencil requires a man in order to be known, so man may require a God in order to be known, and since what he is is self-conscious being capable of realising his own relativity, it seems to me that he cannot know himself without knowing that he is better known than he knows himself.

In other words, evolutionary theory, pursuing its own epistemological exigencies, will have consciously to subordinate itself to a knowing which transcends its own modus. What looked like chance might then turn out to be intelligence which we are endeavouring to recreate and re-enact. What is wrong with Hegel is that he mistakes the recreation for the creation.

The full development of this is, however, no small matter, and I must rest content with these suggestions. I hope, however, that I have made it clear why I think that evolutionary theory can be adequately founded only by epistemological analysis resting on an adequate ontology of human being as being in time.

10 : St Thomas, Newman and the Existence of God

In this chapter I want to do something towards showing the common Christian mind of two very different thinkers, John Henry Newman and St Thomas Aquinas. Both were saintly men of great intelligence expressing the situation of the Catholicism of their times. These were very different indeed. St Thomas wrote within a wide European acceptance of the Faith. Newman wrote within a despised minority, oppressed with a sense of the infidelity of Europe. Newman was driven back upon himself, by a culture which he felt to be inimical, to seek within himself the grounds for personal acceptance of the belief in God. St Thomas could express the common light of a Christian people. Newman belongs to the tradition of men like St Augustine, Pascal, and Kierkegaard, compelled to seek in the heart for those intimations of the reality and presence of God which the things about them seemed often to deny rather than to proclaim.

Let me quote two passages from Newman which seem to me to reflect faithfully the quality of his experience. Speaking of a crowd in a city street he says:

> Every being in that great concourse is his own centre and all things about him are but shades, but a 'vain shadow', in which he 'walketh and disquieteth himself in vain'. He has his own hopes and fears, desires, judg-

ments, and aims; he is everything to himself, and no one else is really any thing. No one outside of him can really touch him, can touch his soul, his immortality; he must live with himself for ever. He has a depth within him unfathomable, an infinite abyss of existence; and the scene in which he bears part for the moment is but like a gleam of sunshine upon its surface.
(PAROCHIAL AND PLAIN SERMONS IV, 82–3)

Or again:

Starting then with the being of a God (which, as I have said, is as certain to me as the certainty of my own existence, though when I try to put the grounds of that certainty into logical shape I find a difficulty in doing so in mood and figure to my satisfaction), I look out of myself into the world of men, and there I see a sight which fills me with unspeakable distress. The world seems simply to give the lie to that great truth, of which my whole being is so full; and the effect upon me is, in consequence, as a matter of necessity, as confusing as if it denied that I am in existence myself. If I looked into a mirror, and did not see my face, I should have the sort of feeling which actually comes upon me, when I look into this living busy world, and see no reflection of its Creator. This is, to me, one of those great difficulties of this absolute primary truth, to which I referred just now. Were it not for this voice, speaking so clearly in my conscience and my heart, I should be an atheist, or a pantheist or a polytheist when I looked into the world.

10 : ST THOMAS, NEWMAN AND ... GOD

> I am speaking for myself only; and I am far from denying the real force of the arguments in a proof of a God, drawn from the general facts of human society and the course of history, but these do not warm me or enlighten me; they do not take away the winter of my desolation or make the buds unfold and the leaves grow within me, and my moral being rejoice. The sight of the world is nothing else than the prophet's scroll, full of 'lamentations, and mourning, and woe'.
>
> (*Apologia Pro Vita Sua*, general answer to Mr. Kingsley, in *Kingsley vs. Newman*, ed. W. Ward, pp. 333–4)

It is clear at once that we are in an entirely different atmosphere from that of St Thomas. What we are reminded of is St Augustine's *abyssus humanae naturae*, Pascal's analyses of the misery of the human condition, and even of Kierkegaard's description of despair. The first personal pronoun, and the admission of personal struggle and misery, are singularly absent from the writings of St Thomas. There are indications, perhaps all the more telling for this absence, for the perceptive person to read, but the strong sense that the world and the body are our home which speaks so clearly in men like St Thomas and Chesterton is absent in Newman.

Chesterton sees the existence of God proclaimed at once in the glory of existence which surrounds a pencil or a post or a tree. All his writing is a celebration of God in creatures. St Thomas, in breaking with the Platonist tradition to the extent which he does, has the same approach.

His rational proofs *a posteriori* that God exists affirm what I may call the congeniality of the common and public world both to the human mind and to God. Hence his acceptance of logic is much easier than that of Newman. He does not find it hard to express things in figure and mood to his satisfaction. Logic prescinds from the personal predicament of each one of us.

Where our concern is primarily with that predicament, we may find logic irrelevant. Logic seeks light and the genius of St Thomas is a genius of light. What Newman seeks is the warmth of the heart in belief. We might say that Newman is seeking the logic of belief, but it is a dialectic worked out in the heart and circumstances of existing individuals. He is, he says, as little able to think by any mind but his own as to breathe with another's lungs. Conscience is nearer to him than any other means of knowledge.

If there is an argument in Newman for the existence of God it is an argument from the testimony of conscience, but we should be careful in what sense we call it an argument. It is rather a persuasion to let the kind of reason which conscience is prevail over the noisy clatter of the argumentative reason. The motto of the *Grammar of Assent* is taken from St Ambrose: *Non in dialectica complacuit Deo salvum facere populum suum*. To rely on mere argument in matters of divinity is gradually to fall into the illusion that God is within our own power.

In the Tamworth Reading Room, Newman criticises Lord Brougham for his insistence that,

One of the most gratifying treats which science affords

us is the knowledge of the extraordinary powers with which the human mind is endowed ... There soon arises a sense of gratification and of new wonder at perceiving how so insignificant a creature has been able to reach such a knowledge of the unbounded system of the universe.

"So," comments Newman,
this is the religion we are to gain from the study of Nature; how miserable. The God we attain is our own mind; our veneration is even professedly the worship of self.
(*Discussions and Arguments*, p. 301)

There is more than a comment on Brougham in these words of Newman. It is a comment on the history of modern philosophy. St Thomas gives rational demonstrations of God's existence, the famous *quinque viae*, and I am prepared to defend these "ways" within the context of St Thomas's mind and situation. But we must consider what happens when we concern ourselves with the proposition that God exists apart from any concern with, belief in or personal acceptance of, God. If we prescind from the latter, there are many respects in which the statement, God exists, is less significant than the statements, oxen exist, or, this piece of iron exists. These statements are empirically verifiable and refer to objects of use. God becomes a concept that we can manipulate, and we will use it to achieve the unity of science or maintain the order of nature. But the day will come when we have no need of that hypothesis, and we will see the mind as the highest moment of reality, as the only governor of nature, and, in its control of the natural order, the only providence.

To state an aspect of the case in Newman's own terminology, assent to the existence of God must be a real not a notional assent, and only to a notional assent will the processes of logical argument lead. The persuasion, to be significant, must be subjective. Objective arguments, he remarks, serve as a vehicle of thought, to open the mind to the apprehension of the facts of the case, and to trace them and their implications in outline, not to convince by the logic of its mere wording.

I am not disposed to think that there is any essential conflict here between Newman and St Thomas. We must never forget that the five ways of St Thomas are a *praeambula fidei*, not a *praeambula scientiae* or *certitudinis* as the proof of the existence of God was for Descartes, or a *praeambula* anything else. In my opinion this radically affects how we must understand the word *praeambula*. Newman's analysis of the relation between faith and reason in the *Oxford University Sermons* contains nothing for a Thomist to reject. Newman is discussing the part which evidences play in the acceptance of God by faith, and he points out that we do not first establish the Gospel truths by rational evidence, and then, by a further and different act, proceed to believe in them. In a manner which reminds one of the opening of the *Contra Gentiles*, and in some ways of Kierkegaard, Newman writes:

> Faith is a principle of action, and action does not allow time for minute and finished investigations. We may (if we will) think that such investigations are of high value; though, in truth, they have a tendency to blunt the practical energy of the mind, while they improve its scientific exactness; but, whatever be their character and consequences, they do not answer the needs of daily life. Diligent collection of evidence, sifting of arguments, and balancing of rival testimonies, may be suited to persons who have leisure and opportunity to act when and how they will; they are not suited to the multitude.
> (X, 188)

Again, he says:
> Hence (faith) is said, and rightly, to be a venture, to involve a risk; or again to be against Reason, to triumph over Reason.
> (XII, 224)

We have to be very careful, however, how we understand reason in the latter citation. In the context Newman means logical arguments on evidences. He does not deny, indeed he brilliantly analyses, the positive part which reason plays in the act of faith, but he points out that it is not a reasoning which starts with clear and distinct ideas but is guided by a complex of presumptions, loves and attitudes of will. He is very clear on the distinction between having a reason and having an argument. The reasons for believing are as complex and unstatable as every person's existential make-up and situation, and Newman will not even try to give a full list of those primary conditions of the mind which are involved in the fact of existence.

Believers, he says,

> may argue badly, but they reason well; that is, their professed grounds are no sufficient measures of their real ones. And in like manner, though the evidence with which Faith is content is apparently inadequate to its purpose, yet this is no proof of real weakness or imperfection in its reasoning. It seems to be contrary to Reason, yet is not; it is but independent of and distinct from what are called philosophical inquiries, intellectual systems, courses of argument, and the like.
> (XI, 212)

What St Thomas is trying to do in the five ways is to find reasons which accord with, but do not substitute for the reasons of faith. The notion of *praeambula* must be seen in connection with the notion of a *fides quaerens intellectum*, and in such an endeavour Newman saw, indeed, a law of the human intellect. He held that in the case of educated minds, investigations into the argumentative proofs of the things to which they have given their assent, are an obligation, or rather a necessity, and that such a trial of their intellects is a law of their nature.

Newman is one of the greatest psychologists of reasoning, especially of moral reasoning. Exquisitely sensible of what went on in himself, one of his great contributions to philosophy is his penetrating descriptions of the manner in which we arrive at our assents, and the variety and subtlety of the subjective factors which come into play in the formation of our convictions. Perhaps nobody else has shown so well the difference between the exercise of the reason in moral matters, which have to do with existential situations, and in matters mathematical and physical, where the reasoning is impersonal and has to do with abstractions.

Readers of Pascal are well acquainted with the distinction which he draws between the *esprit géométrique* and the *esprit de finesse*, the latter having to do with those reasonings of the heart or conscience which are connected with the subtleties of the concrete situation which involve man in the totality of what he is. Pascal's reasons of the heart are not matters of feeling or operations performed by a part of what he is, but the process of appropriating the truth personally. There is a very exact correspondence to this distinction in the differences which Newman exhibits between formal inference on the one hand and natural and informal inference on the other. For Newman, formal inference corresponds to the evidence required by the mathematical and positive sciences, and expresses their demand for a public and impersonal character.

These processes have in a sense an objective existence, and can be detached, as universal procedures, from the subject who operates them. An experiment in a laboratory and, say, the statistical treatment of its results, do not and should not reflect the biography of the experimenter. He has, as it were, to operate for all minds, and his experiments and deductions must in principle be repeatable. The results which we obtain in this manner are very valuable and very necessary for man, but we have always to remember that we obtain them by a recession from the concrete. We deal with concepts which represent only abstract aspects or formalities of things, and we deal with them not as persons but as impersonal technical manipulators. It is by getting rid of the existential complexity both of subject and object that we create a public world of "positive" truth.

For Newman this public world is not enough. We cannot live on the evidences of science because they are bought at the price of abstractness and we live in the concrete world. We distrust speculators and theorists, he says in the *Grammar*, because they are dead to the necessity of personal prudence and judgement to qualify and complete their logic. Science, working by itself, reaches truth in the abstract and probability in the concrete; but what we aim at is truth in the concrete.

Newman points out the difference from those of the positive sciences both of the data of moral reasoning and of the processes by which we reason concerning them. As regards the data, he spoke as follows in his very last lecture in Dublin, given to the Medical School.

> The physical nature lies before us, patent to the sight, ready to the touch, appealing to the senses in so unequivocal a way that the science which is founded upon it is as real to us as the fact of our personal existence. But the phenomena, which are the basis of morals and

religion, have nothing of this luminous evidence. Instead of being obtruded upon our notice, so that we cannot possibly overlook them, they are dictates either of conscience or of faith. They are faint shadows and tracings, certain indeed, but delicate, fragile and almost evanescent, which the mind recognises at one time, not at another, discerns when it is calm, loses when it is in agitation.

(*IDEA OF A UNIVERSITY*, PP. 382–3)

As regards the person himself who reasons, it is difficult to choose among the passages in which Newman expresses the individual and personal character of our apprehensions of truth in the concrete, truth, that is, in which the whole person and his situation are involved. I start with a few sentences torn from a famous passage in the *Grammar of Assent* (p. 213).

Each thing has its own nature and its own history. When the nature and the history of many things are similar, we say that they have the same nature; but there is no such thing as one and the same nature; they are each of them itself, not identical but like ... We call rationality the distinction of man, when compared with other animals.

This is true in logic; but in fact a man differs from a brute, not in rationality only, but in all that he is, even in those respects in which he is most like a brute; so that his whole self, his bones, limbs, make, life, reason, moral feeling, immortality, and all that he is besides, is his real *differentia* in contrast to a horse or a dog. And in like manner, as regards John and Richard, when compared with one another; each is himself, and nothing else, and, though, regarded abstractedly, the two may fairly be said to have something in common, viz. that abstract sameness which does not exist at all, yet, strictly speaking, they have nothing in common, for each of them has a vested interest in all that he himself is; and, moreover, what seems to be common in the two, becomes in fact so uncommon, so *sui simile*, in their respective individualities – the bodily frame of each is so singled out from all other bodies by its special constitution, sound or weak, by its vitality, activity, pathological history and changes, and, again, the mind of each is so distinct from all other minds, in disposition, powers, and habits, – that instead of saying, as logicians say, that the two men differ only in number, we ought, I repeat, rather to say that they differ from each other in all that they are, in identity, in incommunicability, in personality.

As a consequence we all apprehend the truth in different ways and at different times in a manner to which the formal statement or formal deduction of the truth gives us no clue whatever.

> No analysis is subtle and delicate enough to represent adequately the state of mind under which we believe, or the subjects of belief, as they are presented to our thoughts … It is probable that a given opinion, as held

by several individuals, even when of the most congenial views, is as distinct from itself as are their faces. (OXFORD UNIVERSITY SERMONS, P. 267)

Let this be considered, how very differently an argument strikes the mind at one time and another, according to its particular state, or the accident of the moment. At one time it is weak or unmeaning, – at another, it is nothing short of demonstration. We take up a book at one time, and see nothing in it; at another, it is full of weighty remarks and precious thoughts. Sometimes a statement is axiomatic, – sometimes we are at a loss to see what can be said for it. (P. 271)

Now the admission of those circumstances involves a variety of antecedent views, presumptions, implications, associations, and the like, many of which it is very difficult to detect and analyse ... Further let it be considered, that, even as regards what are commonly called evidences, that is, arguments *a posteriori*, conviction for the most part follows, not upon any one great or decisive proof or token of the point in debate, but upon a number of very minute circumstances together, which the mind is quite unable to count up and methodize in an argumentative form ... It is hardly too much to say, that almost all reasons formally adduced in moral inquiries, are rather specimens and symbols of the real grounds, than those grounds themselves. (PP. 273–5)

Now, this apparent nominalism and personalism of Newman's thought may at first sight seem a very far cry from the apparently impersonal "moderate realism" of St Thomas. We must remember, however, that Newman is not writing metaphysics; he is examining how in the concrete the mind reaches its conclusions, and the processes by which a metaphysician's mind concludes are themselves historical and personal. St Thomas in the *Contra Gentiles* reproaches those who, ignoring their fleshly embodiment, "forget that they are men". This is certainly not something which Newman ever ignored or forgot. He points out that the "presumptions" and personally creative character of moral reasoning are not absent in the reasoning of mathematicians and metaphysicians, and he more than suggests that their formal inferences and arguments are simply a convention supervening upon their creative processes in order to make them public.

"How a man reasons is as much a mystery as how he remembers" (p. 259), and if by reducing our reasoning to formal arguments we seek to hide the mystery in the interests of communicability, it remains as its ultimate ground.

> Nothing can be urged, or made to tell, but what all feel, all comprehend, all can put into words; current language becomes the measure of thought; only such conclusions may be drawn as can produce their reasons; only such reasons are in point as can be exhibited in simple propositions; the multiform and intricate assemblage of considerations, which really lead to

judgement and action, must be attenuated or mutilated into a major and a minor premiss. (P. 230)

It may be that at times Newman exaggerates and mechanizes the formalising process, but he has a very strong sense of the creative and personal character not only of moral and religious but also of mathematical and metaphysical reasoning.

> The most remarkable victories of genius, remarkable both in their originality and the confidence with which they have been pursued, have been gained, as though by invisible weapons, by ways of thought so recondite and intricate that the mass of men are obliged to take them on trust, till the event or other evidence confirms them. Such are the methods which penetrating intellects have invented in mathematical science, which look like sophisms till they issue in truths. Here, even in the severest of disciplines, and in absolutely demonstrative processes, the instrument of discovery is so subtle, that technical expressions and formulae are of necessity substituted for it, to thread the labyrinth withal, by way of tempering its difficulties to the grosser reason of the many. Or let it be considered how rare and immaterial (if I may use the words) is metaphysical proof: how difficult to embrace, even when presented to us by philosophers in whose clearness of mind and good sense we fully confide. (P. 217)

In fact, he suggests, the achievements of genius are solitary.

> It is not too much to say that the stepping by which great geniuses scale the mountains of truth is as unsafe and precarious to men in general, as the ascent of a mountaineer up a literal crag. It is a way which they alone can take; and its justification lies in their success. (P. 257)

From this point of view St Thomas's arguments for the existence of God are, in their steps, so many beacons which we observe up the crag of a truth personally reached by St Thomas. They do not cut a highway up which we can casually romp in the manner suggested by some superficial fools who write books on apologetics. Behind the formal proofs we have the dexterity, life, and situation of a real person and perhaps we can appropriate his achievement only in an analogous way.

> Let it be observed, that however full and however precise our producible grounds may be, however systematic our method, however clear and tangible our evidence, yet when our argument is traced down to its simple elements, there must be something assumed ultimately which is incapable of proof. (p. 213)

What is it which is thus assumed? In the *Oxford University Sermons* (pp. 213–14), Newman suggests some of the things which we do assume. He points out that we trust the senses, and the presumption, that the external world, which they reveal, exists. We believe that memory gives us a true report of the past, and assurance of what we hold and do not hold. And we assume the fidelity of our reasoning powers. The matter is amplified in the *Grammar of Assent* in passages which I shall presently refer to. What we assume in fact is our concrete individual being historically situated in the world.

Now, it is to be noticed that the assumptions here recognised by Newman are in fact recognised by St Thomas. Thus in the first proof of God's existence he assumes that we can trust the senses when they reveal to us a world of things in motion. Again, by employing the principle of sufficient reason he is expressing the highest confidence in the rationality of the universe and in the power of the human reason to reach the truth about things.

We can appreciate St Thomas's sense of being firmly seated in history and reality only when we compare his arguments for God's existence with those of Descartes, which are preceded by a doubt of the existence of the external world, of the reliability of memory, and of the power of the reason to reveal the truth about things. Both Newman and St Thomas reject the Cartesian doubt. Both have a basic attitude of acceptance to the world within and without.

It is not always fully appreciated how much is implied in saying that St Thomas's proofs are proofs *a posteriori*. It means that they are proofs from the posture of affairs in which he found himself, and this posture of affairs included a widespread faith that God exists. Consequently he was not trying to reach a new conclusion, or to demonstrate the existence of an entity which nobody had hitherto suspected. His was a faith seeking understanding, and that is why Bertrand Russell can dismiss him as no philosopher on the grounds that he is assuming what he pretends to prove.

I do not wish to try to show here the grounds for holding that faith rectifies rather than perverts the philosophic reason. But I do not wish to deny, I wish rather to suggest, that when St Thomas ends his rational proofs with expressions such as, *et hoc omnes intelligunt Deum*, or, *quam omnes Deum nominant*, the God which we reach is the God in whom we have believed.

When we take away that belief we reach the God who is the guarantor of our physics, or the master clockmaker, but not the God of Abraham, Isaac, and Jacob, not the historical God whom we reach through our sense of location in history. I regard the Thomist proofs as a brilliant effort to express in a rational way this sense of location. It is reason giving an account of where it is, in time and in a body. That is why it is so important to insist that the arguments of St Thomas are not logical but metaphysical arguments. They express an exigency of the thinker, aware of what and where he is, to accept and depend. They state the conditions of my existence here and now, that is, in the very act of my thinking. St Thomas is not trying to find a sufficient reason for the existence of a thinking substance, but of St Thomas in the concrete totality of what he was and believed; and here it seems that his approach has common ground with Newman's approach from individual conscience *ut exercita*.

To put it differently, St Thomas's proofs must be given an existential interpretation. I wonder whether the full flavour of the dictum, *cognitum est in cognoscent per modum cognoscentis*, has as yet been extracted. It might be argued that it should be taken to refer to the mode of human intellection in general, to indicate, for instance, its difference from angelic intellection. Now what Newman does so well is to show not merely how our thinking is conditioned by our human nature, but also how our individual situation and idiosyncrasy affects it. We filter reality through individual temperament, experience and, as we should say now, facticity.

Thinking is the act of a person. Does *per modum cognoscentis* cover this? Let us recall that for St Thomas it is the man who thinks, not a mind unconnected with the body and its history. And as soon as the body is brought into the *cognoscens*, we not only restore the importance of the senses and the imagination, but emphasise our personality as placed, each of us uniquely, in the historical flux. When St Thomas says that man has reason and hands, he is far from Descartes, who could doubt the existence of his hand while he wrote, and who arrives at a thinking subject who is a universal epistemological subject. For St Thomas, thinking is not relative only to the general human condition, but to his own.

If that is so, the proofs of God's existence do not hang in a void of pure reason or spirit, but express the exigencies of a person, endeavouring to make sense of his own situation.

I put these points to Fr Hilary Carpenter, OP, who, in a letter dated 7 June 1960, made the following comment:

> I find myself in entire agreement with you in this interpretation of St Thomas. *Esse uniuscuiusque rei est ei proprium et distinctum ab esse cuiuslibet alterius rei.* (The existing of any thing is peculiar to it and distinct from the existing of any other thing.) The *modus cognoscentis* is precisely commensurate with his being (*esse*), the modification being not only with reference to his nature (*secundum personam*). Actions and therefore passions proceed from his totality (*sunt suppositorum*). I am absolutely certain that not enough emphasis has been laid on the necessary integration of all the elements which go to make up the human *suppositum* or *persona* as actually existing *in rerum natura*.
>
> In the interchange of truth between persons, if the ultimate criterion is objective evidence, this evidence must be clarified commensurately with the individual mode both of the giver and of the receiver. Surely this is what Newman meant. He would not want to deny the basic value of logical science – that is *secundum modum essentialem cognoscentis* (according to the common nature which is in the knower) – but to maintain that clear and objective evidence depends ultimately on the persons concerned – that is *secundum modum personalem cognoscentis* (according to the concrete individual existence of the knower). Logical truth must be commensu-

rate with ontological truth, an adequate representation of it. After all, in its most perfect mode, Truth is a Person. 'I am the Truth.' That is surely how a metaphysical proof differs from a logical one; it must be logical in form, but it is concerned with the actual, not merely objectively but also subjectively.

If this conclusion is true, and I think it is, then a great deal more of the *esprit de finesse* is required both for following and for communicating the arguments of St Thomas than is commonly perceived. To use a distinction of Newman, we have to follow his reason rather than his argument, and reasoning involves what one is. Formal arguments, says Newman, "do but approximate to a representation of the general character of the proof which the writer wishes to convey to another's mind" (p. 275). Hence, he continues, the true office of a writer is

> to excite and direct trains of thought; and this, on the other hand, is the too common practice of readers, to expect everything to be done for them ... and to account every argument as unsound which is illogically worded.

Now what Newman does, in an almost unexampled way, is to draw our attention to the factors involved in finding statements about God subjectively compelling. Newman has very strong roots in the English empiricist tradition, and seems to have had no, or little, acquaintance with the Continental rationalists. While this had at times an adverse effect upon his thought, it made him a keen observer of the human mind in its actual operations, and gave him an extraordinary docility to our constitution as we find it. In the *Grammar* he suggests that we follow Bacon more closely and not distort the faculties of the mind according to the demands of an ideal optimism; we should have regard for modes of thought proper to our nature and faithfully observe them in our intellectual exercises.

What impressed Newman in the course of this faithful observation was the extraordinary number of certitudes with which we operate, such as that Great Britain is an island or that Paris is a city in France or that that is a tree, and what he did in an unprecedented way was to analyse the manner in which we arrive at these certitudes. These certitudes form the solid framework within which we conduct our lives, and are assumed so naturally that we do not stop to take note of their importance. There can, however, be no reform of the mind which does not take account of it as it is, and in its concrete situation.

Bertrand Russell says that he started his philosophical career by asking whether we can know anything for certain. Newman asks on the contrary how it is that we know so many things for certain. Russell is still in the Cartesian tradition, according to which we must commence to philosophise by pressing doubt as far as possible. Newman is aware that such an effort is still historically environed, and is parasitic upon a number of certitudes which we cannot but assume.

> There are some writers who ... lay down as a general

proposition that we have no right in philosophy to make any assumption whatever, and that we ought to begin with a universal doubt. This, however, is of all assumptions the greatest, and to forbid assumptions universally is to forbid this one in particular. Doubt itself is a positive state, and implies a definite habit of mind, and thereby necessarily involves a system of principles and doctrines all its own. Again, if nothing is to be assumed, what is our very method of reasoning but an assumption? and what our nature itself ... I would rather have to maintain that we ought to begin with believing everything that is offered to our acceptance, than that it is our duty to doubt of everything. The former, indeed, seems the true way of learning. In that case we soon discover and discard what is contradictory to itself; and error having always some portion of truth in it, and the truth having a reality which error has not, we may expect, that when there is an honest purpose and fair talents, we shall somehow make our way forward. (GRAMMAR OF ASSENT, PP. 286–7)

Now this somehow making our way forward is a very different and more modest proposal than Descartes's progress by a linear sequence of angelic intuitions, and is much closer to life. It does justice to the multiple conditions of background, temperament, tradition, and environment from which we start, from which we can only intellectually prescind, and through which we must make our way. Existentially we cannot break with these starting points, and we can develop only in and through and out of these. It is only thus that we keep in touch with the concrete, and prevent our lives from becoming the ghosts of themselves.

I shall not go into the question of our certitude of the existence of the external world, important as it is for St Thomas's proof. It has been well dealt with by D'Arcy (*The Nature of Belief*, 2nd ed., pp. 112 ff.). There is a connection between Descartes's doubt of the existence of the external world and his reduction of the self to a ghost of what it is as a living personal existent. I have myself written:

> The failing of Descartes's philosophy is in fact a *lack* of self-consciousness, a failure to respond to the richness of the question, What am I doing? – an escape into an essence in which Descartes ceased to be Descartes. A man's certainty of his existence is an infinitely complex sense of actuality which escapes the clear and distinct idea because of the contingencies in which it is wrapped.
>
> (THE MIRROR OF PHILOSOPHERS, P. 75)

This sense of the concrete character of the self and its destiny is central to the philosophy of Newman. He writes:

> Our being, with its faculties, mind and body, is a fact not admitting of question, all things being of necessity referred to it, not it to other things. If I may not assume that I exist, and in a particular way, that is, with a particular mental constitution, I have nothing to speculate about, and had better let speculation alone. Such as I

am, it is my all; this is my essential standpoint, and must be taken for granted, otherwise, thought is but an idle amusement, not worth the trouble.
(GRAMMAR OF ASSENT, P. 263)

Or again:
I am what I am, or I am nothing. I cannot think, reflect or judge about my being, without starting from the very point which I aim at concluding. My ideas are all assumptions, and I am every moving in a circle. I cannot avoid being sufficient for myself, for I cannot make myself anything else, and to change me is to destroy me. If I do not use myself, I have no other self to use. My only business is to ascertain what I am, in order to put it to use ... My first disobedience is ... to desire to change laws which are identical with myself. (P. 264)

It is impossible to express more clearly than Newman in his chapter on the illative sense that it is the man who thinks and judges, in his concrete situation and with all that he is. "The reasonings which carry us on to truth and certitude are many and distinct, and vary with the enquirer" (p. 270), and he talks of "those first elements of thought which in all reasoning are assumptions, the principles, tastes and opinions, very often of a personal character: which are half the battle in the inference with which the reasoning is to terminate" (p. 274). Hence the famous conclusion:

I am suspicious then of scientific demonstrations in a

> question of concrete fact, in a discussion between fallible men. (P. 312)

St Thomas is, indeed, not the "impartial observer" of reality, and those who describe him as an impersonal thinker should be very careful to qualify what they say. It is true that he is not a personal thinker in the sense in which Newman or St Augustine is. He nowhere describes his sense of personal situation in the manner of the passages which I have quoted from Newman. But he did something more eloquent: he lived it out. He does not appear as an innovator in philosophy in the sense of one who breaks with a tradition, but as a man who makes sense of a tradition by living himself into it and reconciling its conflicting elements. He gives a new value to the past instead of rejecting it as valueless. He places himself in history and in the history of philosophy, whereas Descartes ejects himself from it, formally, of course, though not materially.

The fundamental attitude of St Thomas is not, therefore, one of doubt. It is rather the sense of being tied to beings. We know that there are things which are moved. What lies behind the proofs of the existence of God is the acceptance of things in their limitation, including our own, and also in the concreteness of their actual existence. What the principle of sufficient reason expresses is the insight that neither we nor anything else makes sense unless referred to a sufficient cause which above all must make sense of our actual existence; and the need to make sense of things is not merely a subjective or psychological need, but an ontic need, inscribed in the depths of our being as open to other beings.

It is this acceptance of and openness to being which determines that the proofs shall be *a posteriori*. In a way, St Thomas lies more open to being than even St Augustine. St Augustine argues to the existence of God from the inner nature of the soul. But it would be wrong to say that St Thomas is not also arguing from the nature of the soul. But for him the soul is the form of the body, and expresses its ontological status by gaining knowledge through the senses. Hence his difficulties with his Augustinian contemporaries. Their arguments were too abstract to do justice to things and to men as concrete existences. They were not of their time. It is the ontological proof which seems to him an abstract and *a priori* argument. He wishes to start with bodies and our responses to them through our own.

We must, then, accept ourselves as we are, limited and embodied, and really connected with other beings including sensible beings. We seek to make sense of what we so accept not for the sake of any arbitrary assumption to be proved, but simply in order to be able to accept ourselves as we are. It is something deeper than our theories or our cultural climate which demands it. It is our being in which the principle of sufficient reason is inscribed as a truth of being which requires it.

The proofs of the existence of God are therefore not a method of invention, which is what Descartes required scientific reasoning to be – hence our obsession with new truths and contempt of old – but a formal and deceptively concentrated way of expressing the whole situation of man. They sum up a vast and living experience of our givenness, and by this contact with the concrete do not seem to me to fall within the class of scientific demonstrations which Newman repudiates. It is Descartes's ontological proof which is an intellectual *tour de force* begging the question of the relation of rational and real necessities.

It is the function of philosophy not to discover new truths but to explicitate the truth which is given with us in our own existence. That is why a misdirected doubt can cut the taproot of philosophy. In a sense, a metaphysician can hardly be naive enough, and becoming as a little child is good advice even to philosophers, and perhaps especially to philosophers. One forgets the relevance of St Thomas's simplicity to his metaphysics. Personal characteristics, as Newman has remarked, do come into the picture, and as he further saw, if we are seeking for reasoning, in matters of concrete fact, which dispenses with them, we are chasing a chimera.

Now, children play, and I agree with Mr Michael Mason (in *The Centre of Hilarity*) when he holds that we must regard the metaphysics of St Thomas as a game. Play, he says, is conflict creatively controlled by a containing order. For the philosophy of St Thomas, he writes,

> the end was in the beginning and in a true sense all the answers were known in advance. It was a true game. In fact, the very form in which his greatest philosophical work was constructed is a highly formalised expres-

sion of play – the vigorous play of medieval disputation, a sort of chess of argument; the pattern of objection, solution and conclusion in the articles of the *Summa* reproduces in a highly abstract form the kind of serious and lively game which Socrates and his friends initiated in the dialogues recorded by Plato.

Had Kierkegaard, who admired Socrates for the right reasons, seen this connection, from the perception of which his ignorance of medieval philosophy debarred him, he would have been spared some pitfalls. He had the humorous sense of incongruity and the comic necessary for a metaphysician.

It is necessary in reading the proofs of St Thomas to remember that there *are* underlying attitudes and that there is a containing order. This is only to remember that philosophy is an activity of men and not of pure spirits like Bertrand Russell. Principally, there is the attitude of humility in the face of being. We cannot pretend that we can dispense with it. If we do, pride surreptitiously creeps into its place. If we do not accept the existence of God on the evidence of our finiteness, we shall fall into the sin of Lucifer, which is the charge which Kierkegaard brings against Hegel. Kierkegaard was saved from the solemnities of speculation by his sense of humour. He could not have been so serious if he did not see that it was funny to be a man.

In a way, then, we are accepting what we are trying to prove: our finiteness and dependence, shown to each one of us here and now, which are inexplicable and meaningless apart from the existence of God. One has to be a devil to take oneself seriously, and St Thomas is showing that one can't. Philosophers too often remind me of the Satanic conclave in *Paradise Lost*. If we are not well disposed towards our own being, and towards that of God, we shall never prove his existence and may have some difficulty with our own. If we do not find the latter funny we shall end up by finding it absurd in the Sartrean sense.

Let me end, then, by returning again to the part which will plays in our knowledge. I have spoken about being well disposed to being, and I suppose it is because he is well disposed that St Thomas is accused of assuming what he wishes to prove. I have tried to indicate in what sense this is a philosophical virtue and not a vice. But I should not leave the subject without some mention of what St Thomas says about connatural knowledge.

> We can give the name of natural love to this selective affinity (*connaturalitas*) which inclines a thing toward what suits it. (E. GILSON, THE CHRISTIAN PHILOSOPHY OF ST THOMAS AQUINAS, P. 273)

Now, what suits the mind is truth which is discerned in being, and what attracts the mind to being is love. That is why we draw truth into ourselves and subjectively appropriate it. We cannot know what we will not love.

We have through love to set up relations in being which are the presuppositions of any cognition. Lovableness is not our subjective addition to a thing but a quality of being, and not to love certain things is not to take up an impartial and "scientific" attitude towards them, but to cut ourselves off from their being and render ourselves incapable of knowing what they are. It is a sort of castration of the intellect.

I remember seeing a famous physiologist pushing electrodes into a moribund chameleon and saying sarcastically: "Of course, we scientists love animals!" True enough, he did not love the chameleon in the concrete, but he did love it as a physiological diagram, and he did love his own knowledge. But he had cut the chameleon off from nature, and his own knowledge from his wider humanity. To be impartial he had to make both the animal and himself partial, that is, less than they were, and I am prepared to argue that the highest knowledge is partial in another sense. It has to be based on a plentitude of love which will not be satisfied with less than the whole of ourselves in a concrete and full relationship to what is known.

We cannot know God unless we are prepared to love him, and behind the proofs of St Thomas there is a living man whose faith sought understanding. I know how many quibbles can be raised about this statement by pseudo-Thomists who see in the proofs the triumph of a sort of disembodied philosophical intellect, but I have tried to show that the *a posteriori* character of the proofs gives the lie to this. A saint who brushes his teeth is still a saint when he does it, and so is he when he rationally proves God's existence. It is an act which is located in his total existence, and I suspect that it is really this total existence which is the assumption which some of his critics consider to invalidate the proof.

However, as Newman affirms, there is no proof for anyone outside his assumption of what he is, and what we make of St Thomas's proof will depend on what we consider to be the degree of his fidelity to the nature of existence, and his own existence. If proof requires that we get outside ourselves, there will be no proof. The most valid argument in these matters is that which most fully expresses the fidelity of the intellect to itself, and our intellect is not a disembodied intellect. In the last resort, and this is what Newman so clearly saw, every man must achieve his own certitude, and whether he finds St Thomas's proof valid or not depends on what he brings to it: the whole of himself in his contingency, or something less. It is not the worse for that.

It wasn't St Thomas who wished to do other people's thinking for them, although so many behave as if he had done so. It is the man that thinks, not a disembodied mind, and if a man does not find his humanity and his world meaningful, but can survive on thinking that they just are, he will not find the proofs convincing. To say that they are valid or invalid is an existential affirmation involving what each of us is. It is not the conclusion of an abstract logic. We cannot fire them at anyone with a gun, for to get them across requires that tact, that prudence, that sensitivity to persons and situations which Aristotle considered to be the main requirement for the practical man. This accounts for the excellent section on Aristotle's *phronesis* in the *Gram-*

mar (pp. 268 ff.). Art as well as logic make the metaphysician.

Both Newman and St Thomas start with me moving a pencil. St Thomas, perhaps, lays more emphasis upon the pencil than upon the me; Newman upon the me. But they complement and do not contradict each other. Newman helps us to see that certitude is an act of living mind in its totality, and convinces me, at any rate, of the futility of regarding the Thomist proofs as a technical *tour de force*, or of raising merely technical objections to them which do not do justice to the wider qualities of the man who presented them.

Is it men who convince, or arguments? The error lies in dissociating them, and in concrete matters at any rate conviction is produced by the good man with the good reason. In the last resort, the death of Socrates convinces more than his arguments, and what captivates me about St Thomas is that he was well disposed towards pencils. He would have died rather than be a Manichaean, and if he illuminated the universe with his pencil it was because he allowed its being to speak in the humble Brother Thomas. The proofs are merely what the pencil had to say.

One of the problems raised by this is the problem of *witness* to truth. Newman says that instead of trusting logical science we must trust persons. In order to understand this we must remember that Newman never played fast and loose with truth. He is not telling us to stop thinking, or to be satisfied to take things on authority, though there are many occasions when we do and must. What he is saying is that truth, or at any rate some kinds of truth, are best discerned in persons, persons who, as Kierkegaard would say, are in the truth.

At first sight his statement would appear to be very far from the advice given by St Thomas to students, never to allow personalities to interfere with our judgement, but to attend solely to the truth of what is said. Now, obviously St Thomas's advice is excellent. Perhaps most of our entrenched prejudice, and the untruths in which we remain, are due to the fact that we are unwilling to read or listen to people who for some or other reason we consider to be *non gratae*. But I do not think that this means, or that St Thomas wished to say, that personality has nothing to do with truth.

Suppose that owing to this or that influence we have an indifference or even an animosity towards a certain philosopher. Then suppose that we decide to give him a fair hearing – and observe how often this happens because someone we trust has advised us to. We then discover that he has said a number of things which are true, and which enter into our thought and become part of us. Insofar as that happens we feel him to be a friend, an alter ego. Our judgement about him changes, and we discern that he is in the truth when formerly we thought he was not.

Truth is not something which has nothing to do with friendship and personal affinity. What St Thomas is saying is that friendship depends on truth and not truth on friendship. Those who are most worthy of friendship are those who have integrity, and those who have integrity are those who are true to themselves and true to reality. What unites us to others is a common view of reality which is in accordance with it. When we feel well disposed towards someone, there is a presumption that he is in some measure in the truth, but the only test is reason; and we must not forget that owing to our subjective perversities we are often ill-disposed towards people *because* they are in the truth. That was the source of the prejudice against Socrates. The only test of truth is reason.

When Newman says: instead of trusting logical science, we must trust persons, is he discounting the test of reason? I do not think so. I admit that in the *Grammar* he is unduly hard upon abstract thought and formal inference, but that is not from a distrust of reason, but because he had a polemic against those who had too exclusive a view of the manner in which truth is gained. He realised that truth is not the conclusion of an argument but a hold upon the concrete, and that reasoning is not done by a machine but by a man. The fact that we can construct electronic brains would, I think, have been used by Newman to point his argument. He would have said that a machine can logicise, but not reason.

An electronic proof of the existence of God would not make much impression on us. What impresses us is the assent given to this truth by a man, whose reasons for it are not formal deductions from selected data, but the convergence of his total experience as a rational being. For Newman, too, the test is reason. He is not telling us to make truth dependent on personalities, but advising us that the whole truth depends on a whole person. It is grasped by him in the totality of his concrete situation, so that in the last resort it is the total person, and not a method or calculus or other logical construction, which is the criterion of truth. That is what he means by trusting persons, and I can see no divergence between him and St Thomas on this point.

Truth, at any rate in philosophic and theological matters, is not separable from behaviour. That is the solid conviction behind Plato's affirmation that to know the good is to be a good man. It is only too easy and frequent to give an over-intellectualist interpretation of his statement. We observe behaviour in following any philosophical argument. We ask whether the proponent is honest, whether he has put forward all the data, whether he is credulous or emotional, whether he has jumped to a *non sequitur*, and so on. He must, in short, show integrity in his reasoning, and in this sense there are always moral reasons behind our assent to an argument.

In the last resort we believe a man for what he is, a fact which makes a tremendous demand upon the teacher of philosophy. What is important is not to have a philosophy but to be a philosopher. Philosophy is exercised within the context of life, and it is a good, that is, a true philosophy when it draws into itself the whole of that context by reason, and makes it correspond with the total reality. Life then becomes a witness of reality, that is, it takes on the quality of truth.

When Socrates died for his philosophic conviction, it

is not enough to say that his death shows that he believed what he said. A fanatic or a lunatic may be sincere in that sense, and his actions may make us believe in his sincerity without in the least convincing us of the truth of what he holds. But what Socrates in fact does is something more. He sets a seal upon the truth of what he held, and lifts it from mere subjectivity. It would be a long matter to set out fully the grounds for saying this. But what we observe in his action is that it makes sense of his life, and that it displays not merely sincerity but integrity – for a very sincere man may be very divided and disintegrated.

Further, it makes sense not only of his inward life but, since outward and inward cannot be divided, of a slice of Athenian history, and of the events and men whom he knew. He died as he had lived, that is, he followed the logic of the concrete, which was always the controlling factor of his speculations. His death is the conclusion of a piece of concrete logic, reflected in the mind by the *Phaedo* and other dialogues, but whose *quod erat demonstrandum* had to be an act because its logic was the logic of history which is superior to the logic of mathematics.

Let me say, however, that I do not think that philosophical achievements like St Thomas's proof ever become historically dated, any more than the thought of Socrates, and that not in spite of but *because* they were so true to the man and his times. They do not merely make logical sense: they make sense of a man and his surroundings. History is truer than physics or mathematics, and we have to bring our historical sense, our sense of the concrete, and our experience of ourselves and of persons to bear in matters where validity depends not only on formal considerations, but on the nature of existence which unfolds itself to us through time and history.

In any search for truth what is important is that a man should not bluff himself. He must be open to being and his own being. This being is moving and if St Thomas ascends from the moving to the unmoved it can only be from the point at which he stands. At that point we can never stand. In this sense the proof is existentially rather than logically necessary. If it convinces us of the necessity of integrity to our situation in a world of motion and history, it is a valid proof, even perhaps when it forces us to disagree with it. It is because men matter more than thoughts that it is so indestructible.

In the last resort it is only man's search for integrity which leads him to assert the existence of God. He is looking for his sufficient reason in the times and conditions in which he lives. That is the full bearing of the statement that the principle of sufficient reason is a principle of concrete being. So we are again at the point where Newman and St Thomas come together. We must trust persons and our own person rather than logic, and if we trust St Thomas it is precisely not because he speaks to us as a timeless authority, but as one who makes us aware of our own condition and the need to make sense of it. You cannot dissociate the timely and the timeless, and that is the essence of the proof.

Bibliography of sources quoted

Anon, *The Cloud of Unknowing*.
Aquinas, St Thomas, *Summa Theologica*; *De Veritate*.
Arabian Nights, tr. Powys Mathers, Folio Society, bk. IV, 1958.
Augustine, St, *Confessions*; *City of God*; *Commentary on St John's Gospel*; *On Music*; *On the Trinity*.
Barfield, Owen, *Saving the Appearances*, Faber, 1957.
Bowman, A.A., *A Sacramental Universe*, Princeton, 1934.
Buber, Martin, *The Legend of the Baal-Shem*, Harper, 1956.
The Buddhist Scriptures.
Carpenter, Fr Hilary, ms. letter to author.
Carson, Rachel, *The Edge of the Sea*, New American Library, 1959.
Chuang-tzu, *The Way of Chuang-tzu*, anthology by Thomas Merton, Unwin Books, 1970.
Descartes, R., *Opera Omnia*, Adam-Tannery, 1966.
Emerson, R.W., *Society and Solitude*.
Feuerbach, L., *The Essence of Christianity*, 1.x. viii, tr. George Eliot, Harper Torchbooks, 1957.
Gilson, E., *The Christian Philosophy of St Thomas Aquinas*, Gollancz, 1957.
Goldbrunner, J., *Cure of Mind and Cure of Soul*, Notre Dame, 1963.
Heschel, A.J., *The Passion for Truth*, Secker & Warburg, 1974.
Hobbes, Thomas, *Leviathan*, esp. 1.6; 1.8; 1.10.
Hume, D., *Essays, Moral and Political*, 1741.
Hume, D., *Treatise of Human Nature*, ed. L.A. Selby-Bigge, Oxford, 1951.
Hyers, M. Conrad, *Zen and the Comic Spirit*, Rider, 1974.
James, St, *The Epistle of St James*, 4.1–3.

Johnson, Samuel, *Rasselas*, ch. 3.
Jung, C.G., *Modern Man in Search of a Soul*, Routledge & Kegan Paul, 1961.
Lao-tzu, *The Way of Life (Tao-te-Ching)*, Wildwood House, 1974.
Maritain, J., *Science and Wisdom*.
Marrou, H., in *Cross Currents*, xi. 1. 1972.
Mason, Michael, *The Centre of Hilarity*, Sheed & Ward, 1959.
Merleau-Ponty, M., *Phénoménologie de la Perception*, Gallimard, 1945.
Miller, H., *Science and History*, Berkeley, California, 1939.
Newman, J.H., *Complete Works*, esp. *The Grammar of Assent*; *Parochial and Plain Sermons*; *Apologia pro Vita Sua*; *Discussions and Arguments*; *Oxford University Sermons*.
Patanjali, *The Yoga Sutra*, tr. Swami Venkatesananda, Chiltern Yoga Trust, Elgin, 1975.
Plato, *Symposium*; *Republic*; *Gorgias*.
Prabavanananda, Swami, *The Spiritual Heritage of India*, esp. bk. IV, Allen & Unwin, 1961.
Reyburn, H.A., *Hegel's Ethical Theory*, Oxford, 1921.
Saurat, D., *Death and the Dreamer*, London Westhouse, 1946.
Stern, Karl, *The Flight from Woman*, Allen & Unwin, 1966.
Suzuki, S., *Zen Mind, Beginner's Mind*, Walker/Weatherhill, 1970.
Traherne, T., *Centuries of Meditation*.
Upanishads, tr. R.E. Hume, Oxford, 1934.
Versfeld, M., in *The Nature of Philosophical Enquiry*, Notre Dame, 1970.
Watts, Alan, *The Way of Zen*, Thames & Hudson, 1951.
Weiner, H., *The Kabbala Today*, Collier Books, 1969.
Wiesel, Elie, *Souls on Fire*, Weidenfeld & Nicolson, 1972.